80s Guitar Classics

AUTHENTIC TRANSCRIPTIONS WITH NOTES AND TABLATURE

This publication is not authorised for sale in
the United States of America and/or Canada

HAL LEONARD EUROPE
Distributed by Music Sales

Exclusive Distributors:
Music Sales Limited
8/9 Frith Street, London W1V 5TZ, England.
Music Sales Pty Limited
120 Rothschild Avenue, Rosebery, NSW 2018, Australia.

Order No. HLE90000550
ISBN 0-7119-7828-X
This book © Copyright 1999 by Hal Leonard Europe.

Unauthorised reproduction of any part of this publication by
any means including photocopying is an infringement of copyright.

Cover design by Michael Bell Design.
Photography by George Taylor.
Guitar kindly loaned by Rhodes World of Music.
Printed in the USA.

Your Guarantee of Quality:
As publishers, we strive to produce every book to the highest commercial standards.
The book has been carefully designed to minimise awkward page turns and
to make playing from it a real pleasure.
Particular care has been given to specifying acid-free, neutral-sized paper made from
pulps which have not been elemental chlorine bleached.
This pulp is from farmed sustainable forests and was produced with
special regard for the environment.
Throughout, the printing and binding have been planned to ensure a
sturdy, attractive publication which should give years of enjoyment.
If your copy fails to meet our high standards, please inform us and we will gladly replace it.

Music Sales' complete catalogue describes thousands of
titles and is available in full colour sections by subject, direct from Music Sales Limited.
Please state your areas of interest and send a cheque/postal order for £1.50 for postage to:
Music Sales Limited, Newmarket Road, Bury St. Edmunds, Suffolk IP33 3YB, England.

www.internetmusicshop.com

Addicted To Love… Robert Palmer… 4
Cult Of Personality… Living Colour… 11
Every Breath You Take… The Police… 19
Eye Of The Tiger… Survivor… 22
Heat Of The Moment… Asia… 26
Heaven's On Fire… Kiss… 32
Hit Me With Your Best Shot… Pat Benatar… 37
Money For Nothing… Dire Straits… 41
Oh, Pretty Woman… Van Halen… 51
Pretending… Eric Clapton… 58
Pride And Joy… Stevie Ray Vaughan… 66
Sunday Bloody Sunday… U2… 75
Sweet Child O' Mine… Guns N' Roses… 79
You Give Love A Bad Name… Bon Jovi… 88
You Shook Me All Night Long… AC/DC… 93

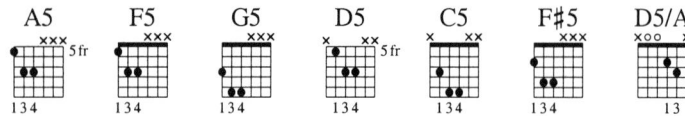

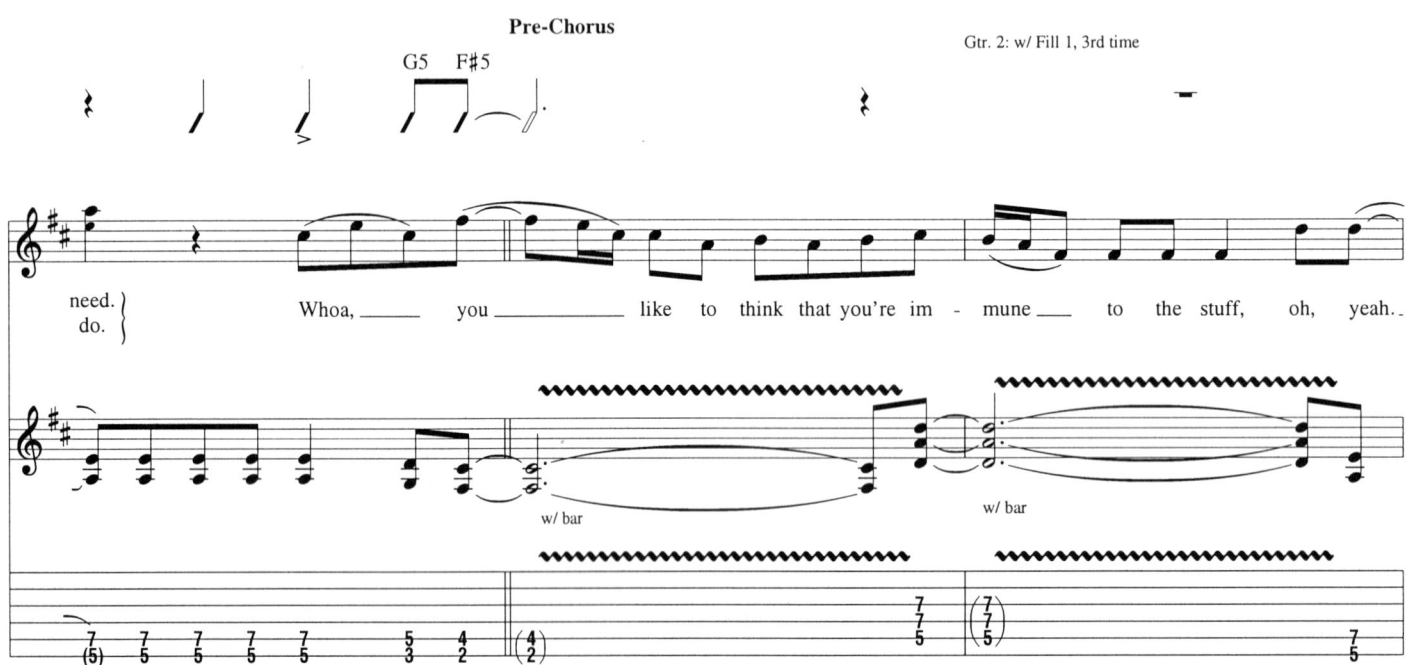
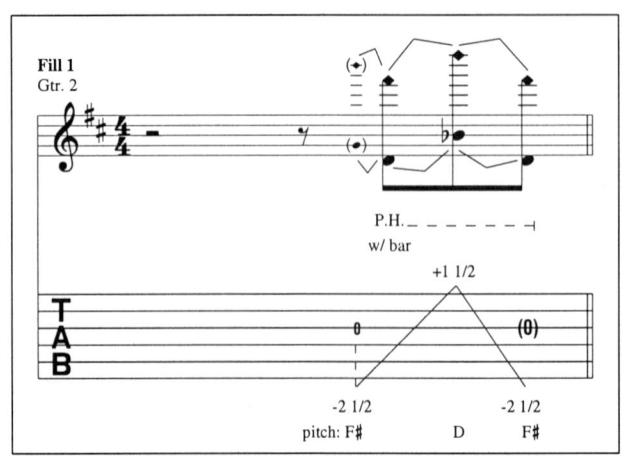

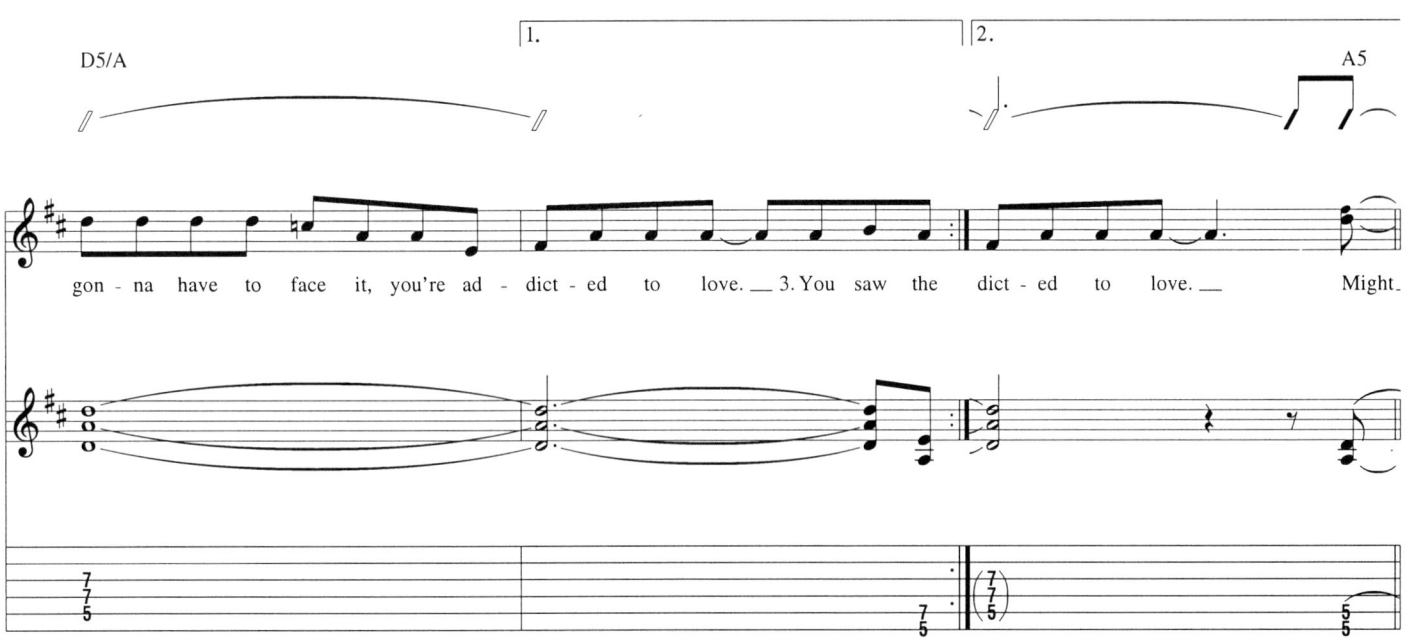
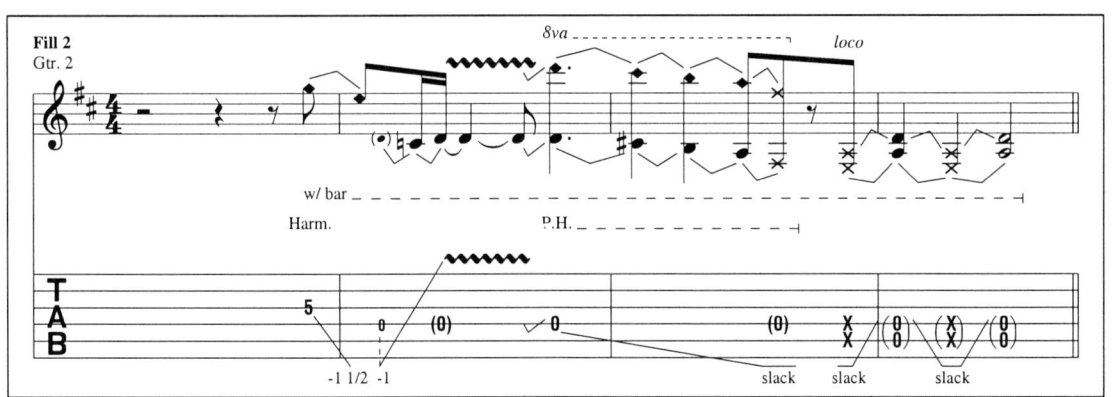

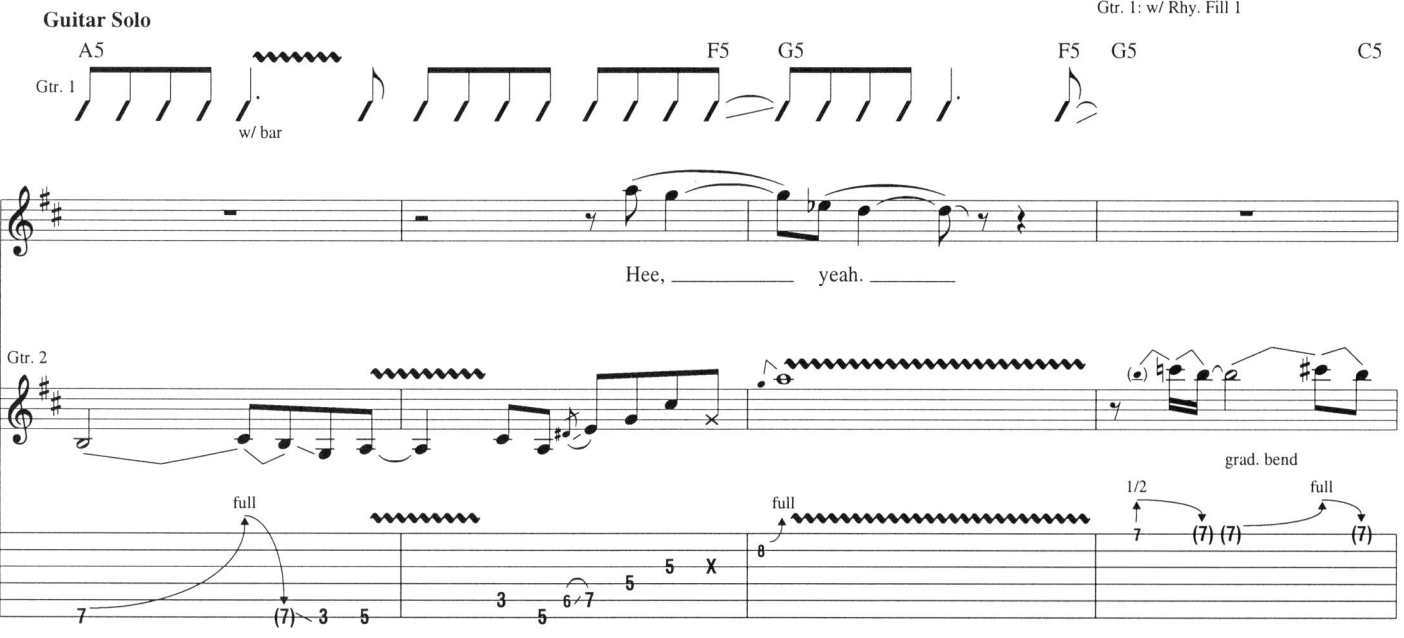
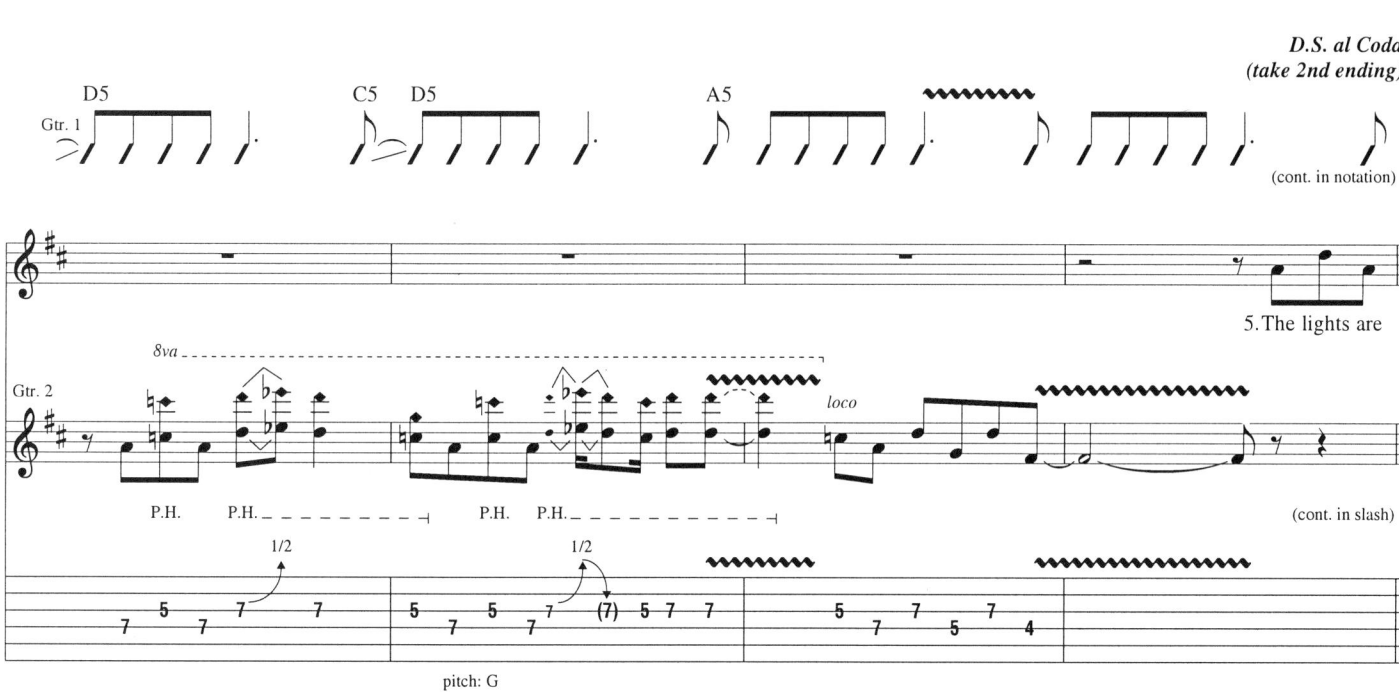
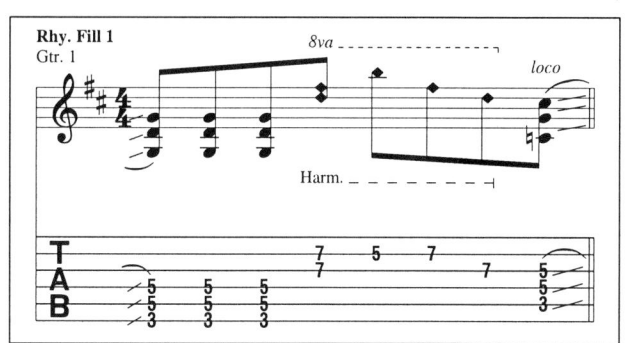

9

Additional Lyrics

5. The lights are on, but you're not home.
   Your will is not your own.
   Your heart sweats, your teeth grind.
   Another kiss and you'll be mine.

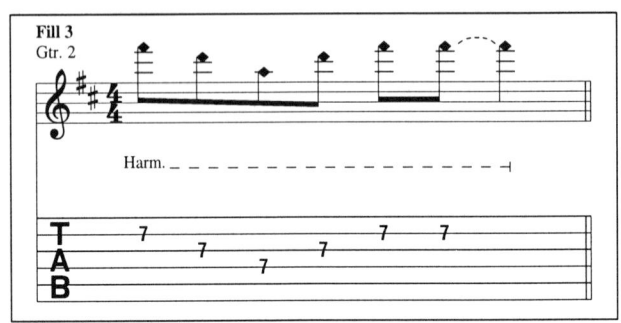

Cult of Personality

Words and Music by William Calhoun, Corey Glover, Muzz Skillings and Vernon Reid

Spoken: "And during the few moments that we have left, we want to talk right down to earth in a language that everybody here can easily understand."

Copyright © 1988 by Dare To Dream Music, William Calhoun, Corey Glover, Muzz Skillings and Famous Music Corporation
All Rights Controlled and Administered by Famous Music Corporation
International Copyright Secured   All Rights Reserved

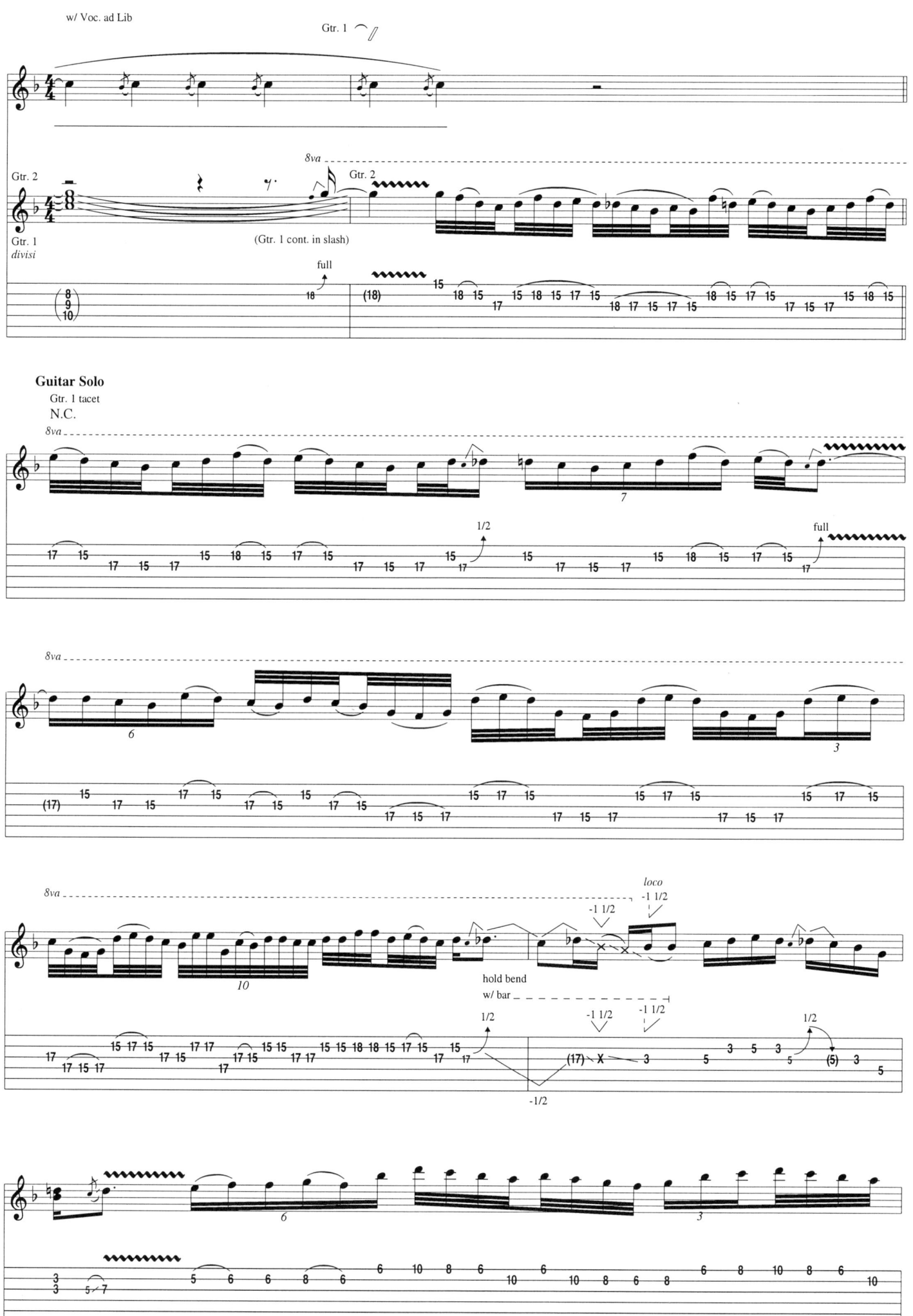

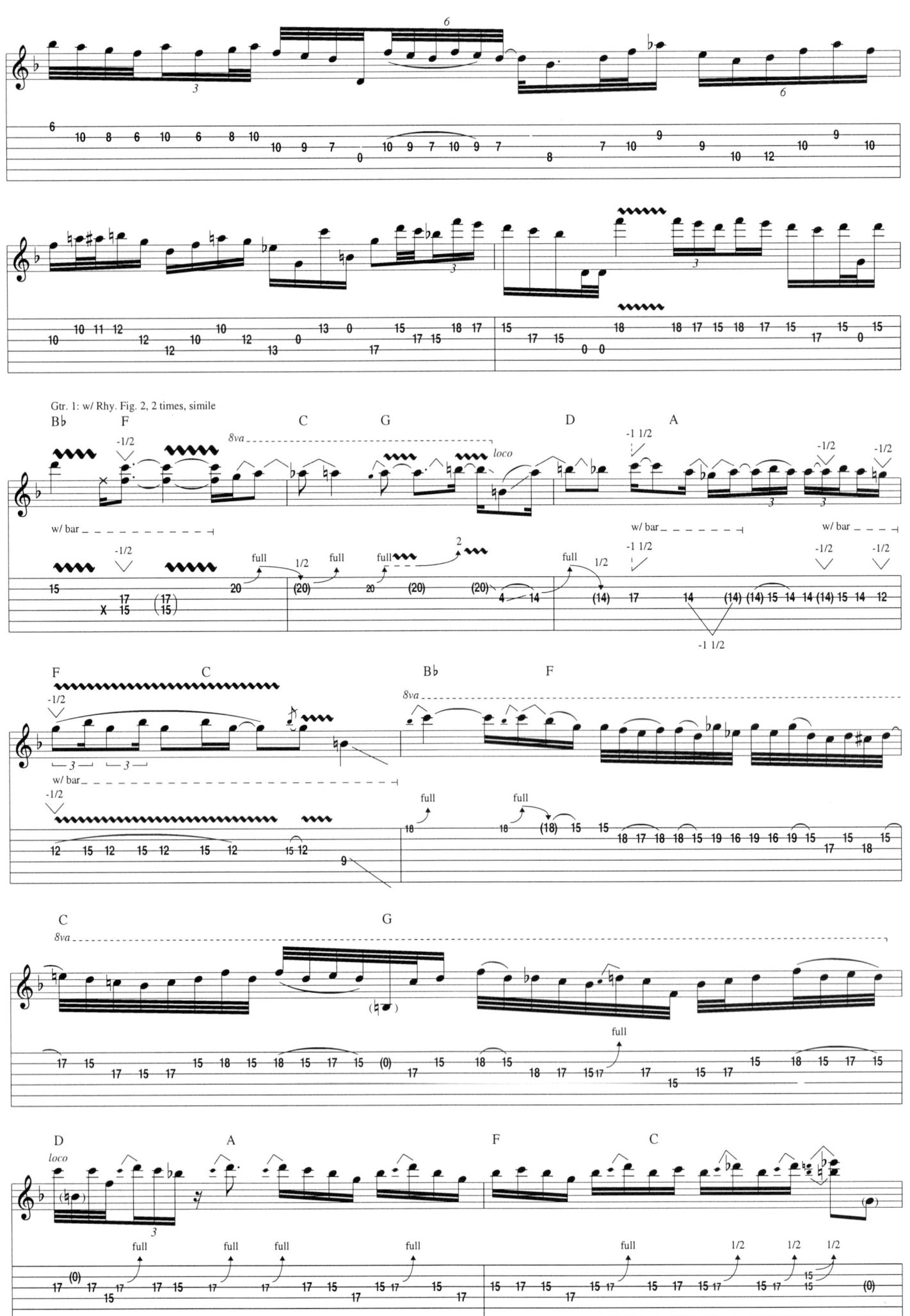

1.
Dsus2
Esus2
F♯m9
Ooh.
Ooh.
P.M.
2.
Aadd9
D.S. al Coda
Ooh.
Oh, can't you
Coda
Dsus2
Esus2
Ev-'ry move you make. Ev-'ry step you take, I'll be watch-ing you.
Gtr. 1
F♯m9
I'll be watch - ing
Outro
(w/ ad Lib lead voc.)
Aadd9
F♯m9
Dsus2
Play 8 Times & Fade
you.
I'll be watch - ing
1., 5. (Ev-'ry breath you take. Ev-'ry move you make. Ev-'ry bond you break. Ev-'ry step you take.)
2., 4., 6., 8. (Ev-'ry sin - gle day. Ev-'ry word you say. Ev-'ry game you play. Ev-'ry night you...)
3., 7. (Ev-'ry move you make. Ev-'ry vow you break. Ev-'ry smile you fake. Ev-'ry claim you stake.)

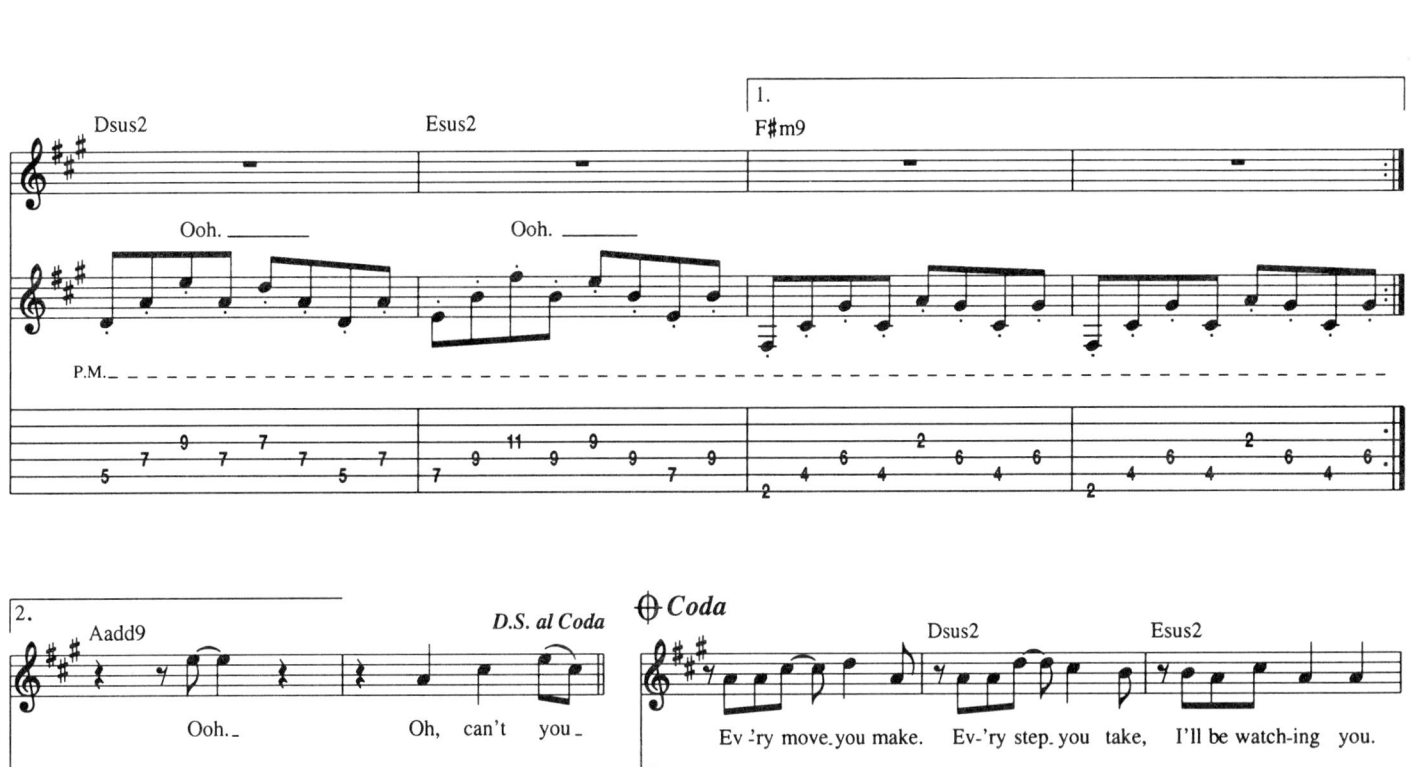

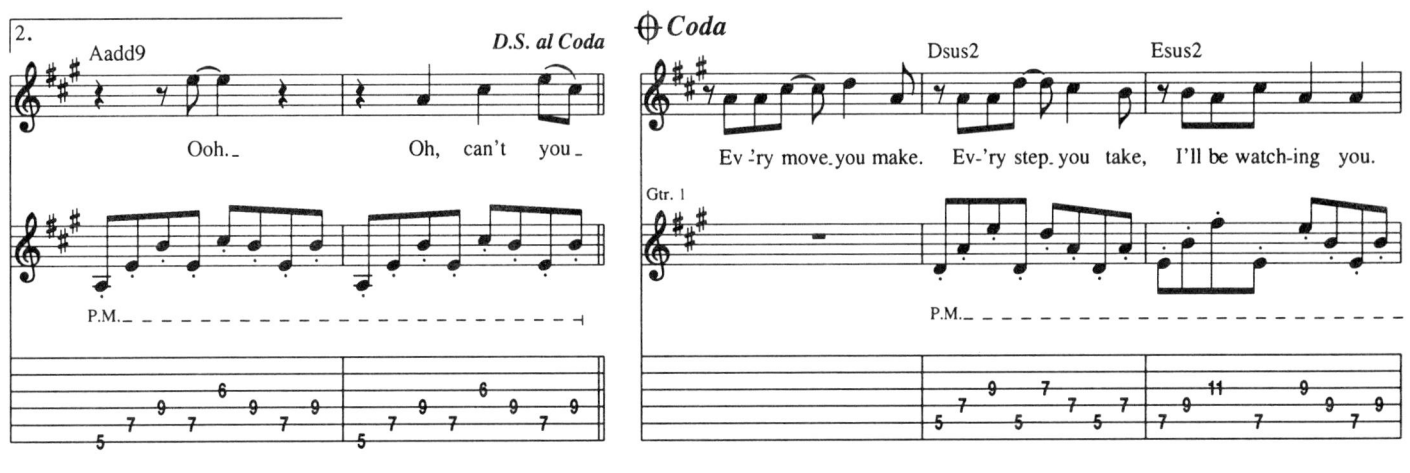

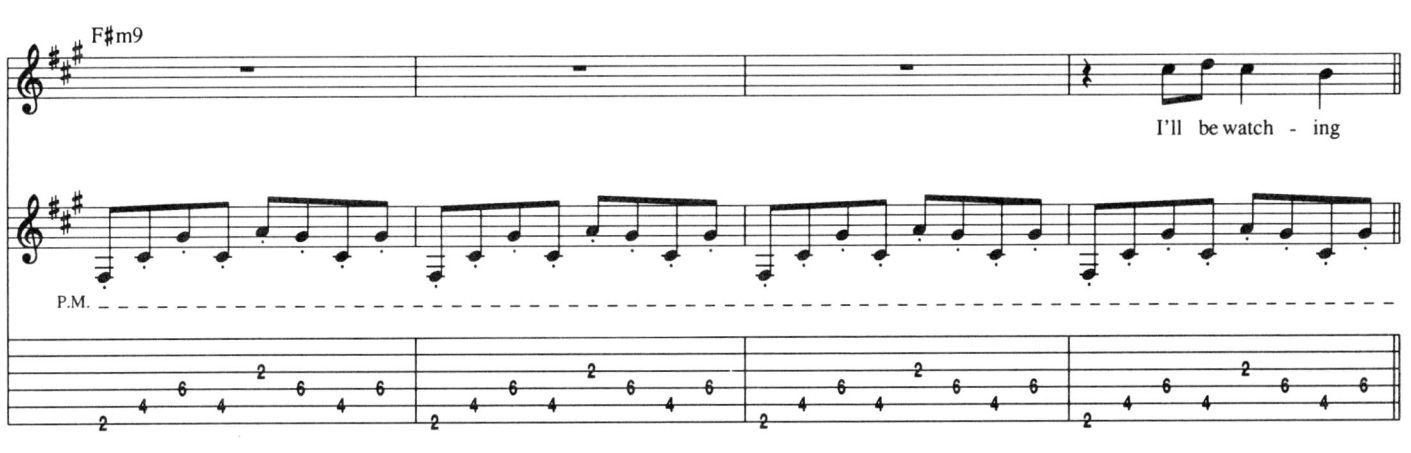

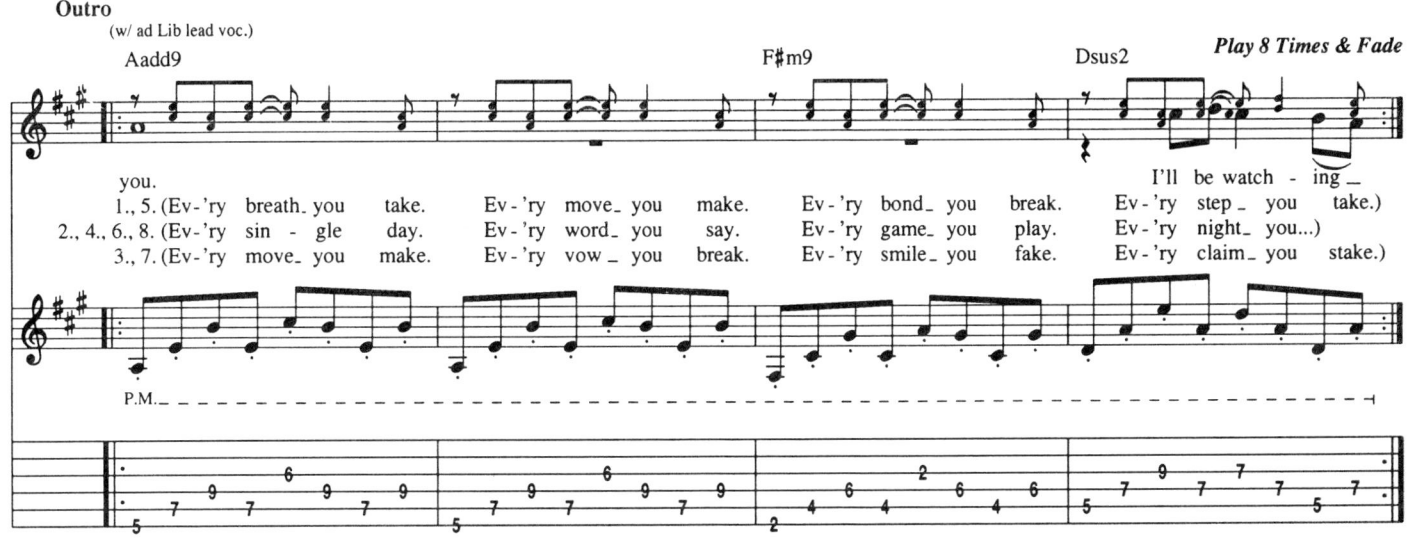

Eye of the Tiger

Theme from ROCKY III
Words and Music by Frank Sullivan and Jim Peterik

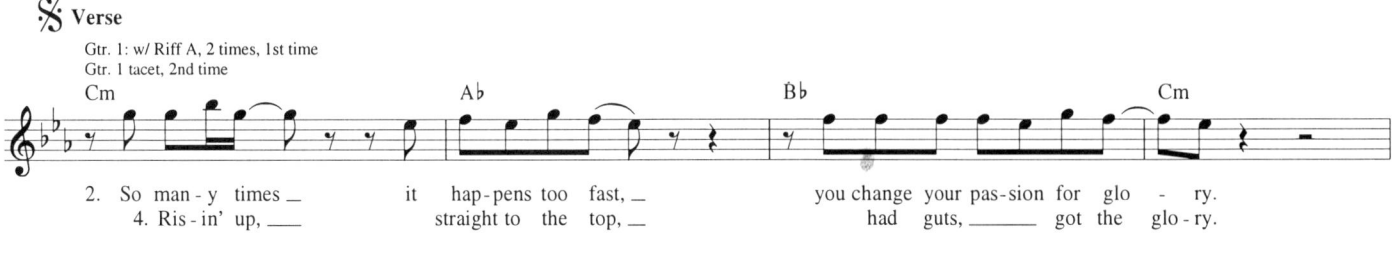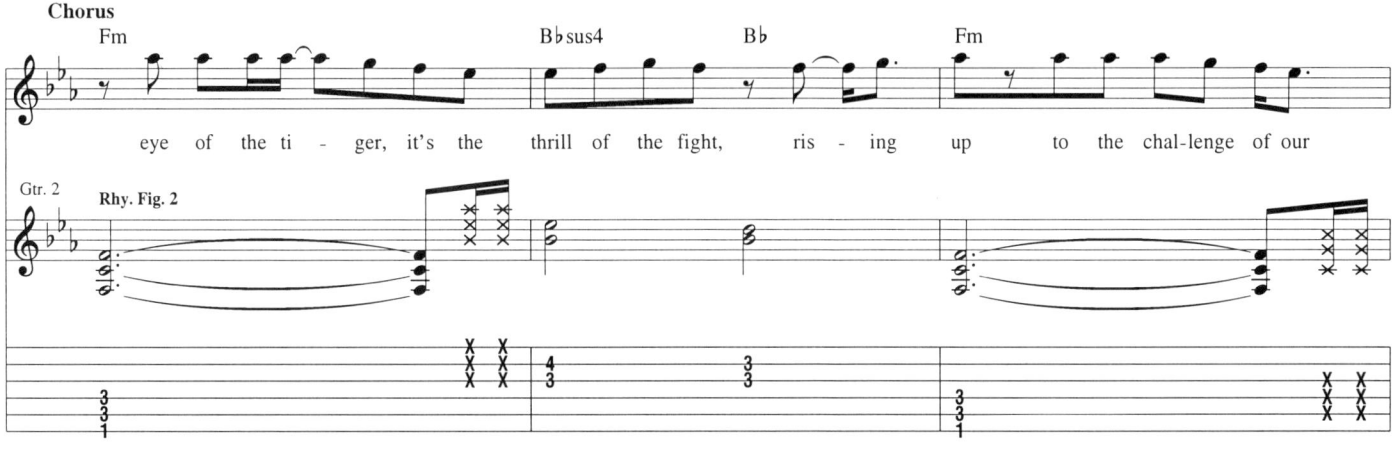

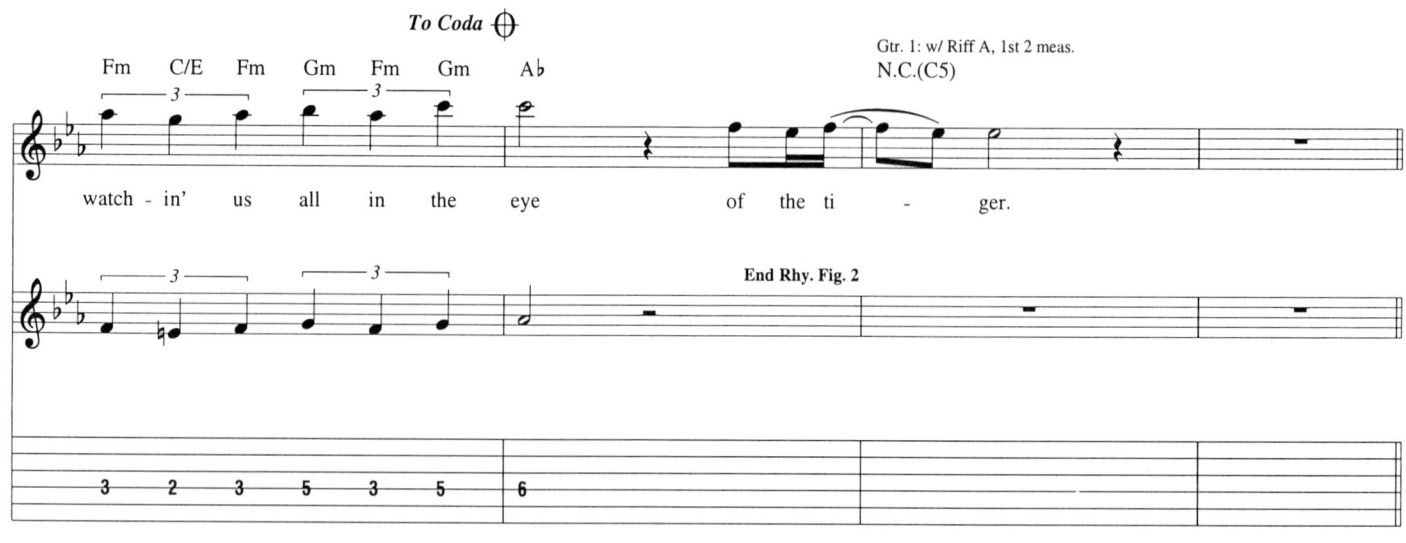

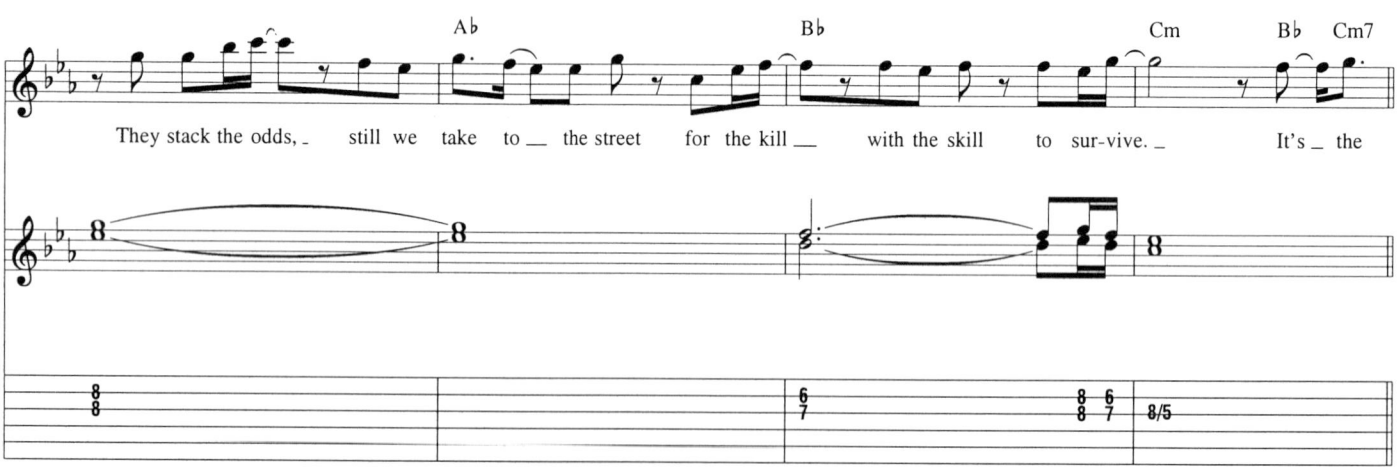
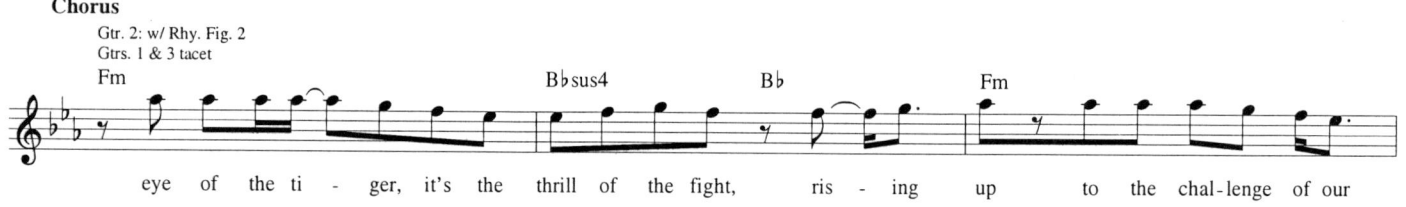

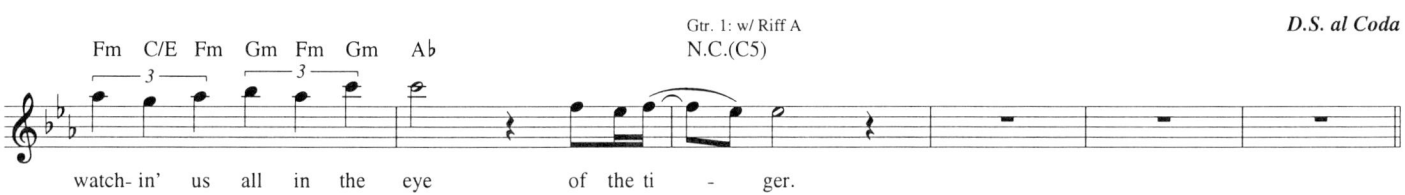

Coda

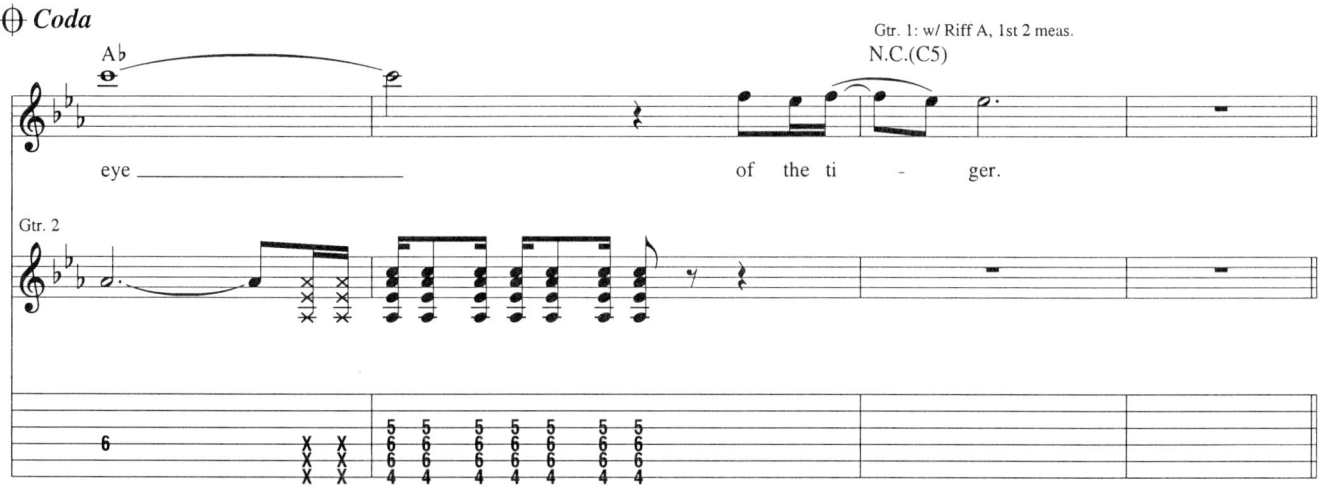

Outro

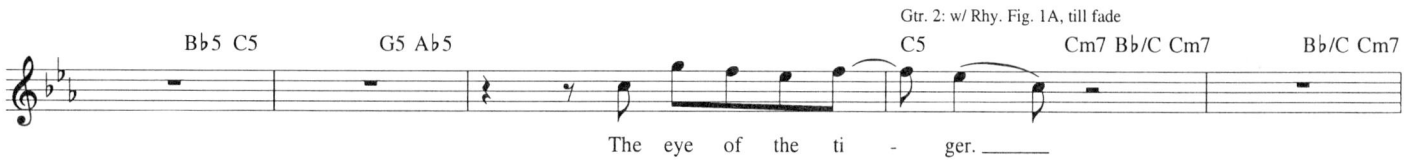
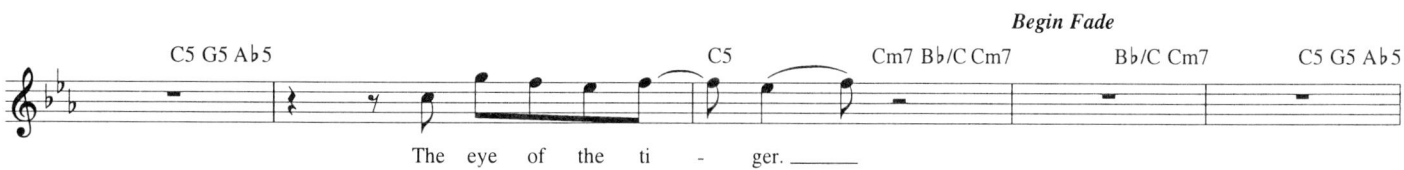
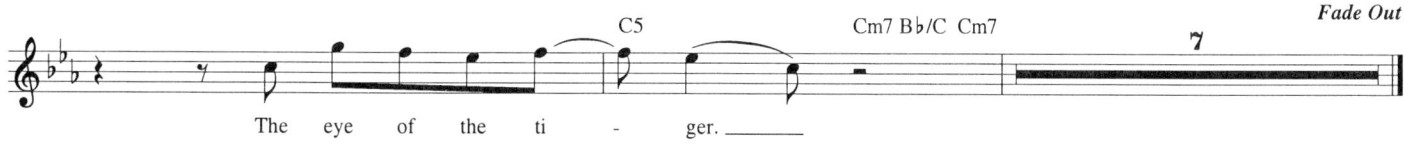

Heat of the Moment

Words and Music by Geoffrey Downes and John Wetton

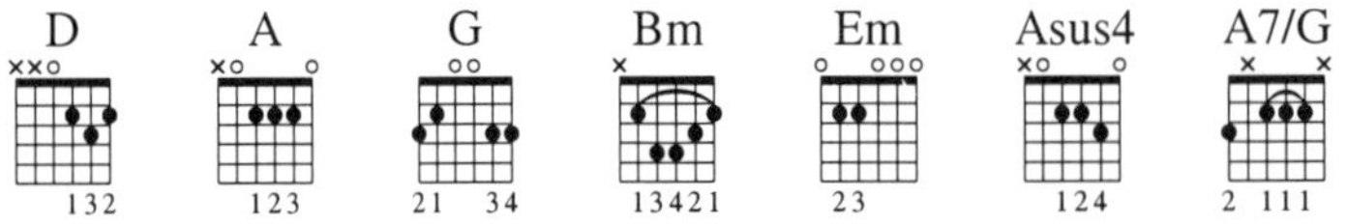

Tune Down 1/2 Step:
① = E♭ ④ = D♭
② = B♭ ⑤ = A♭
③ = G♭ ⑥ = E♭

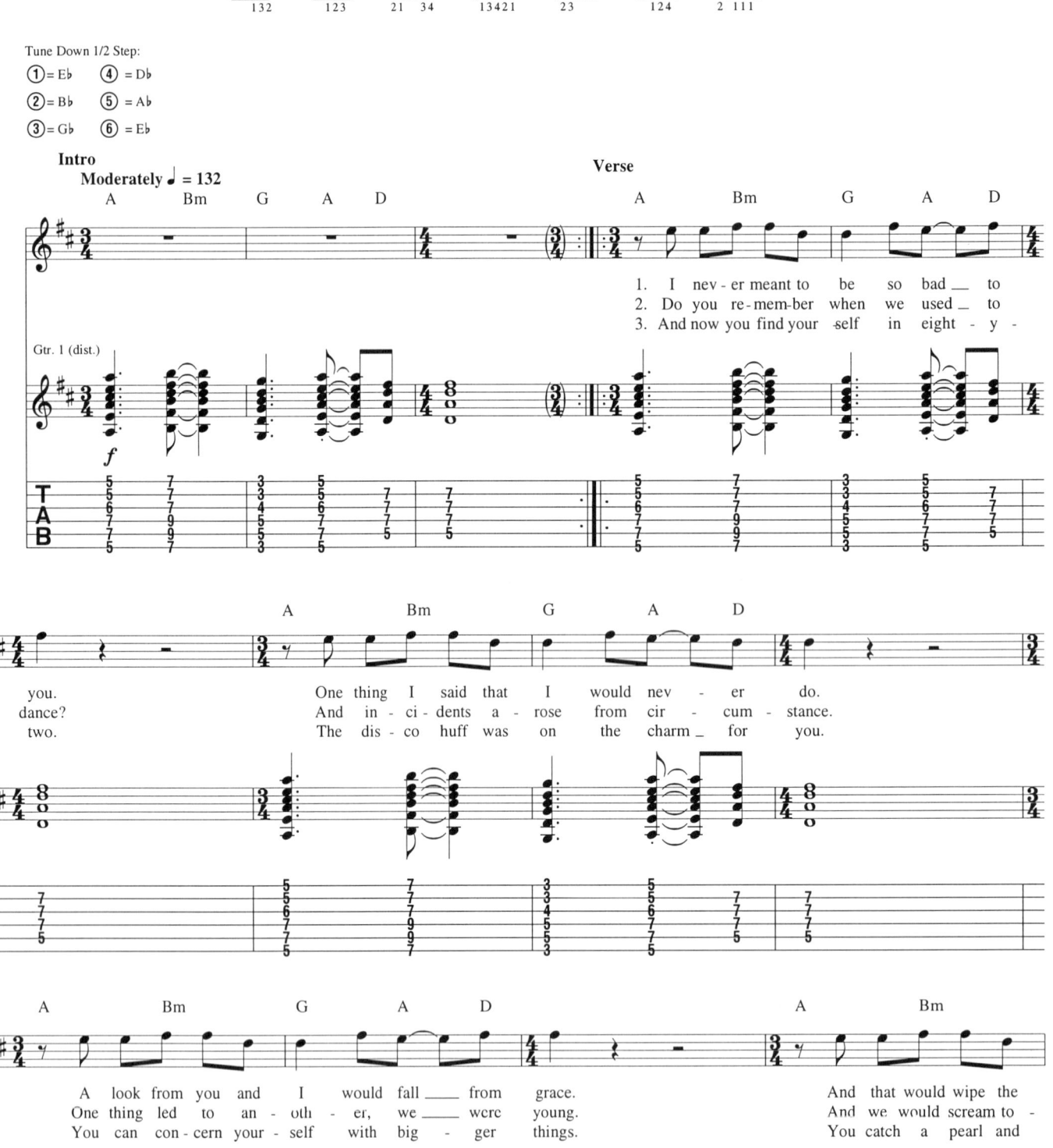

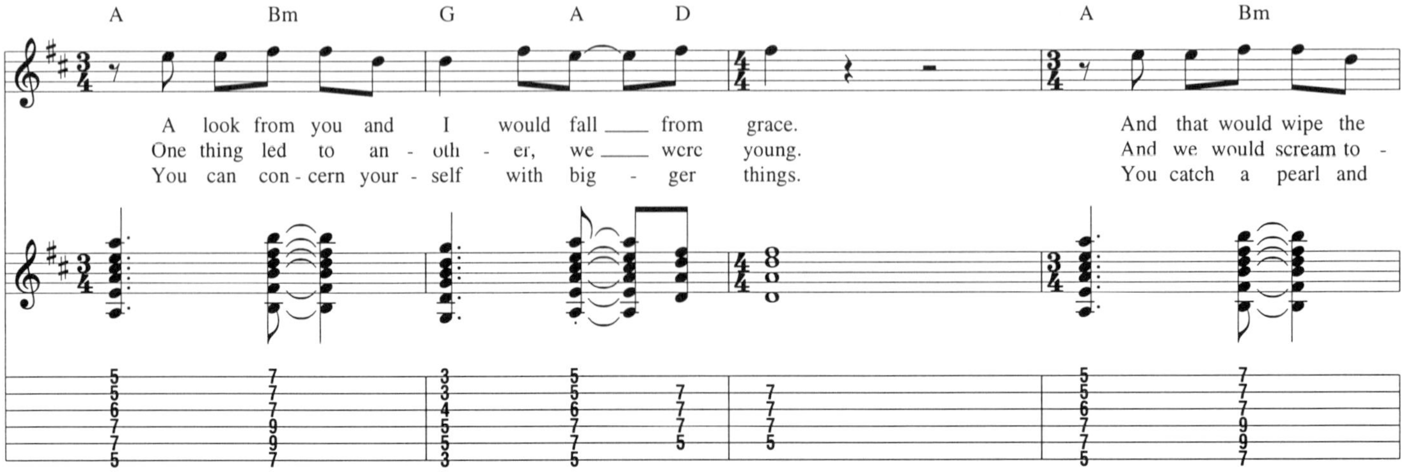

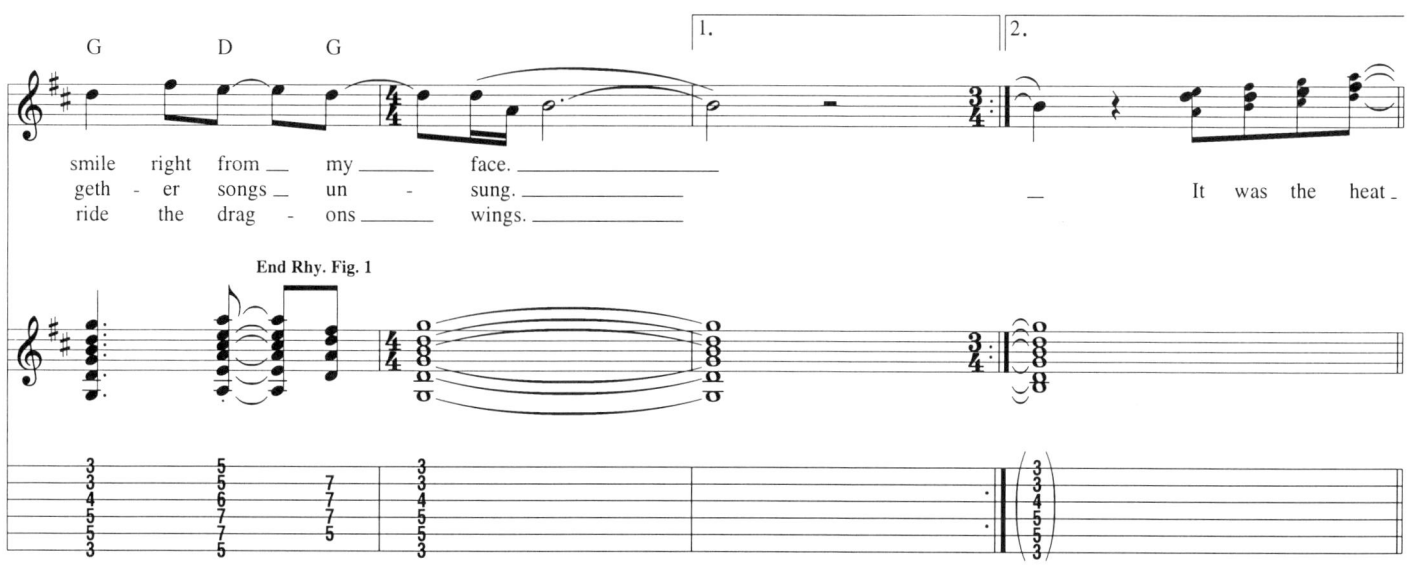

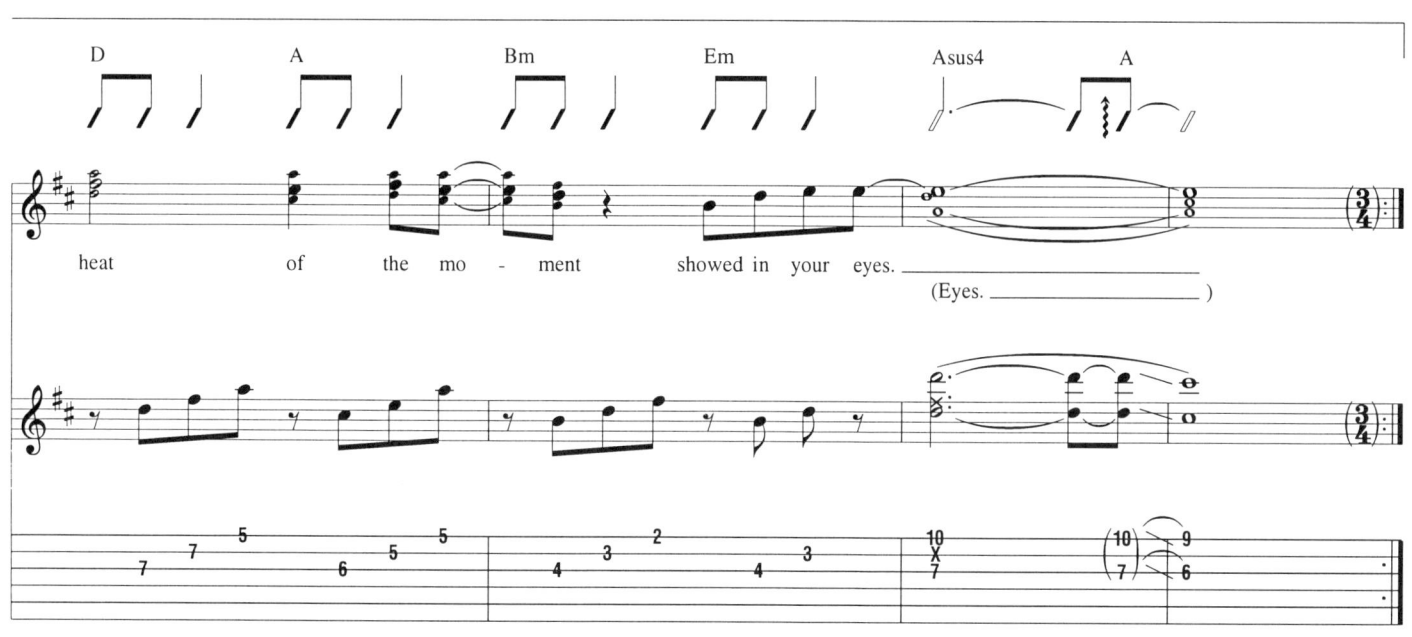

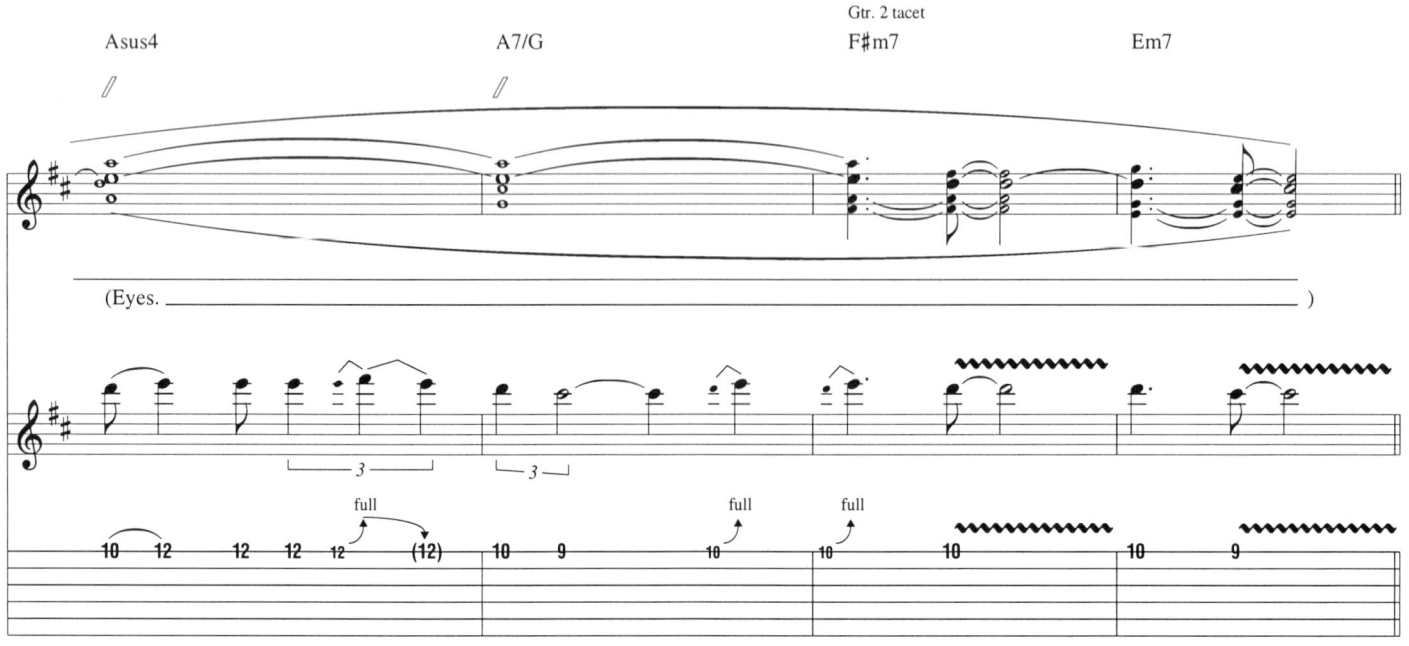

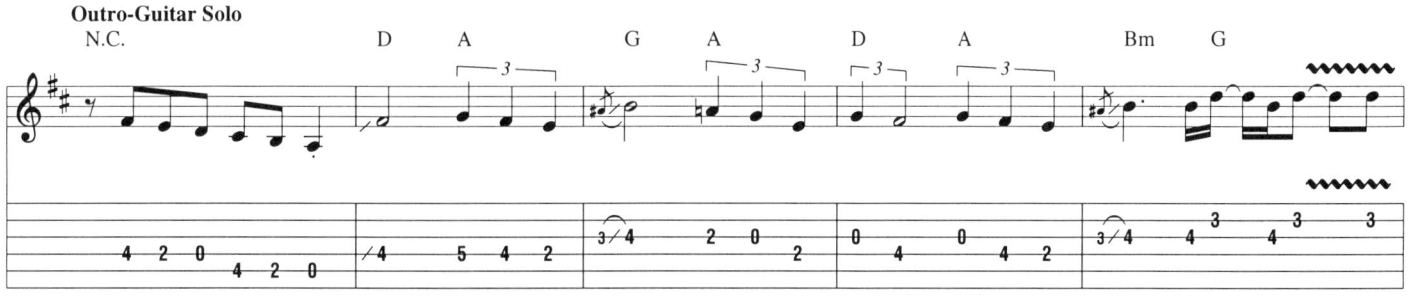
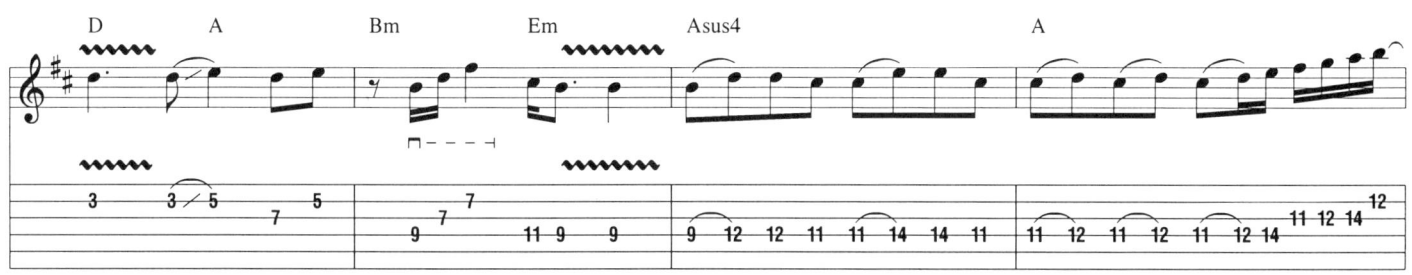
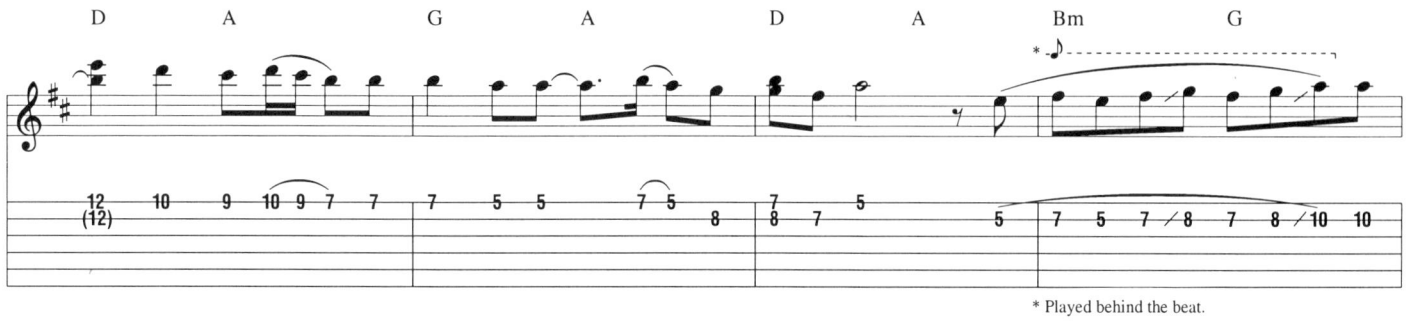
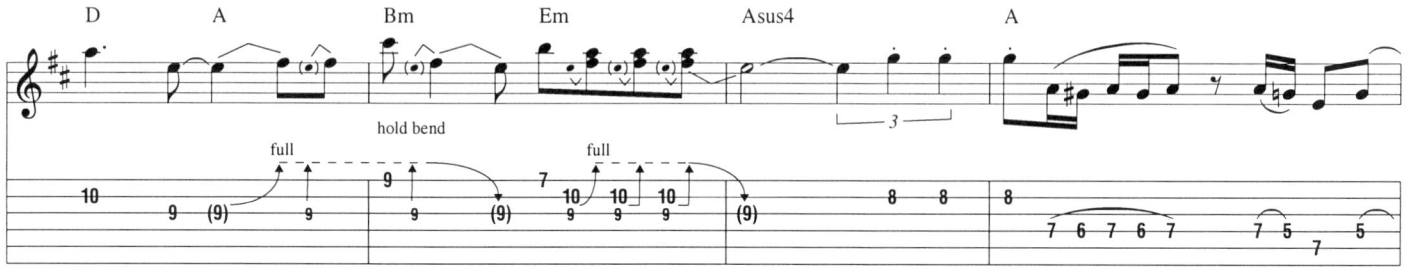
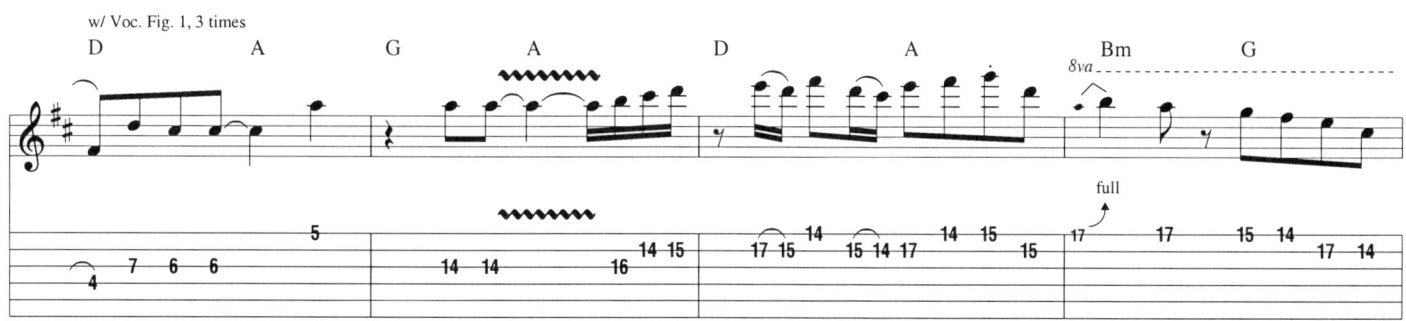
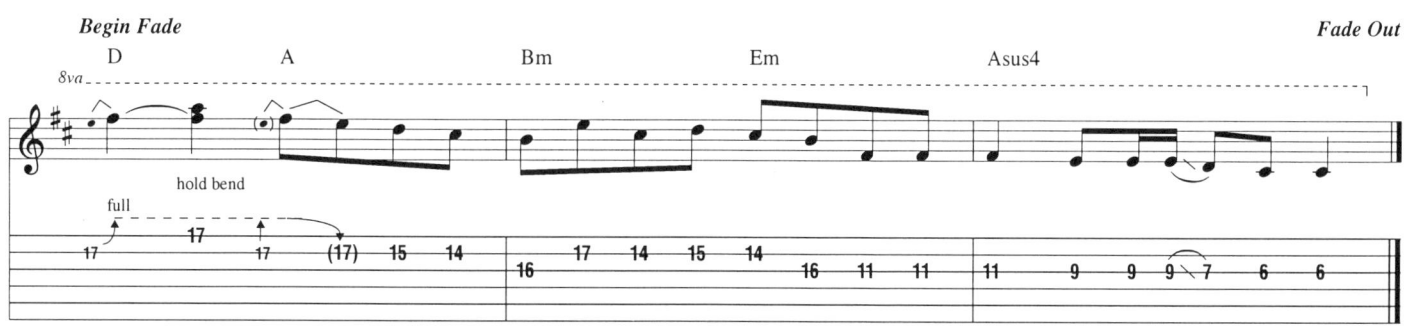

Heaven's On Fire

Words and Music by Paul Stanley and Desmond Child

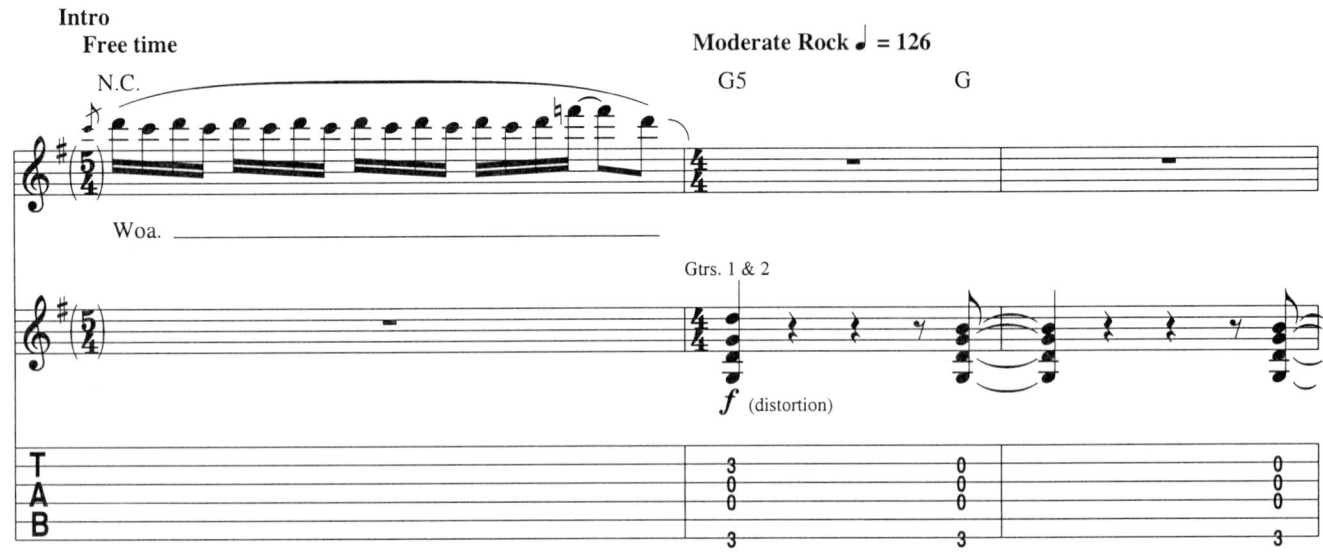
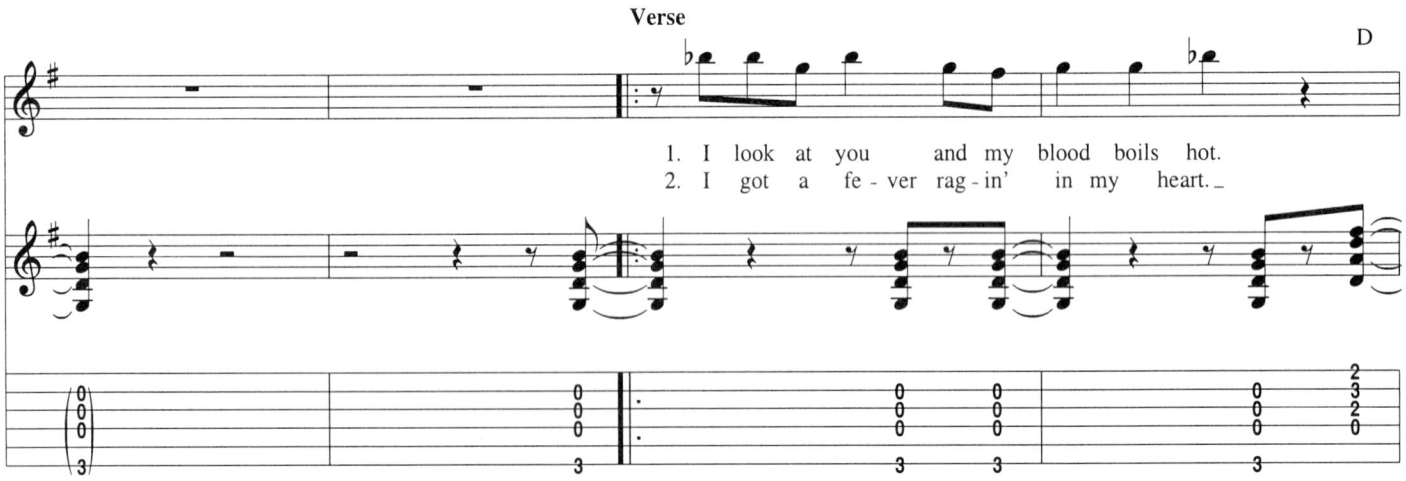
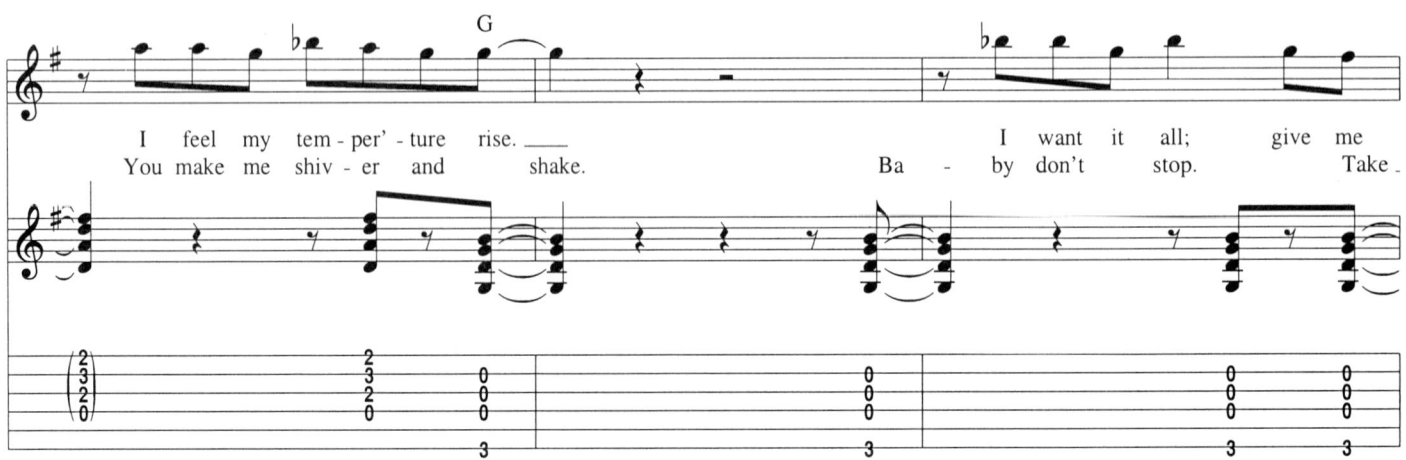

Copyright © 1974 Hori Productions America, Inc. and Desmobile Music Co., Inc.
All Rights Administered by PolyGram International Publishing, Inc.
International Copyright Secured   All Rights Reserved

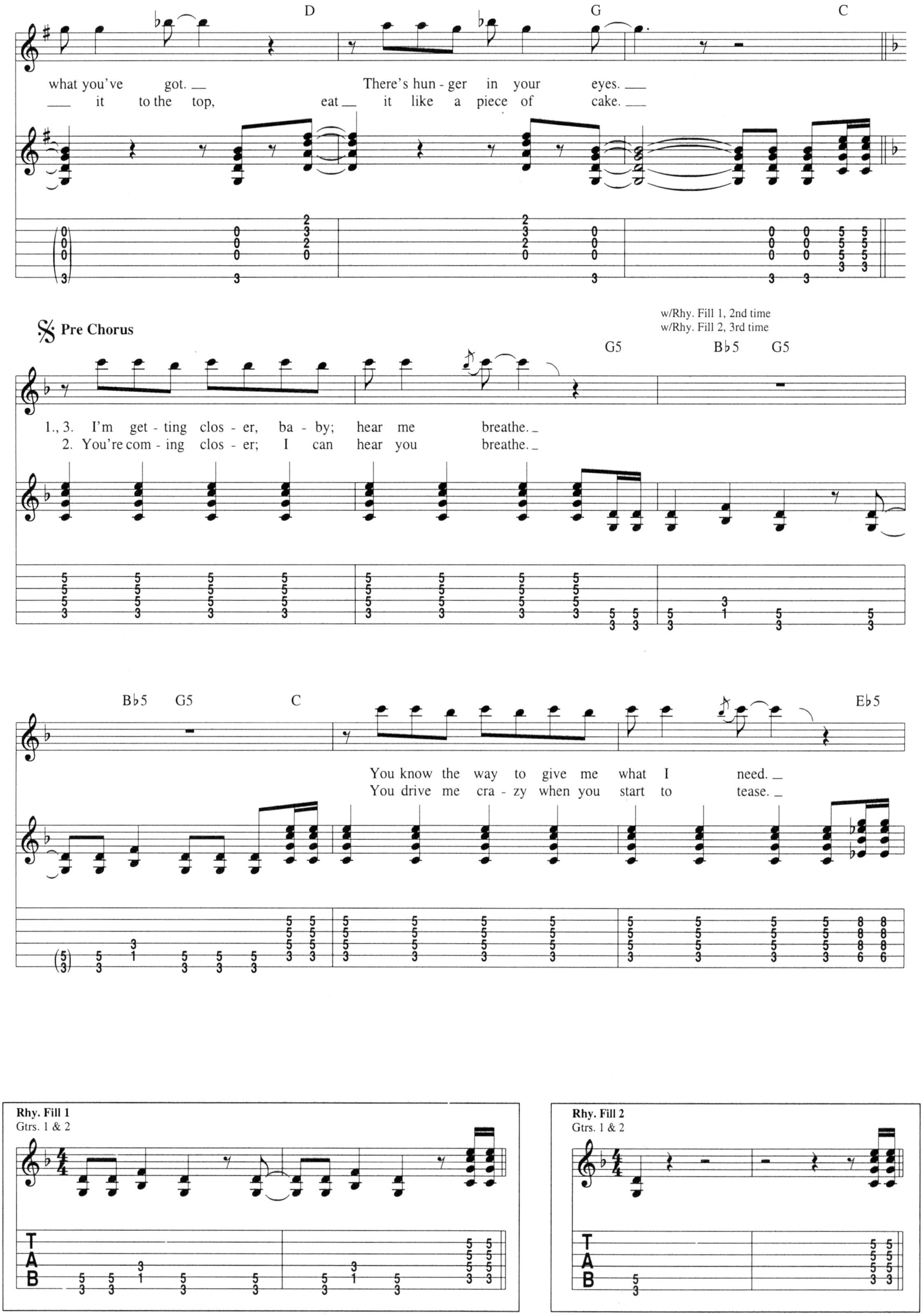

what you've got. There's hun-ger in your eyes.
___ it to the top, eat it like a piece of cake.

%S Pre Chorus

w/Rhy. Fill 1, 2nd time
w/Rhy. Fill 2, 3rd time

1., 3. I'm get-ting clos-er, ba-by; hear me breathe. ___
2. You're com-ing clos-er; I can hear you breathe. ___

You know the way to give me what I need. ___
You drive me cra-zy when you start to tease. ___

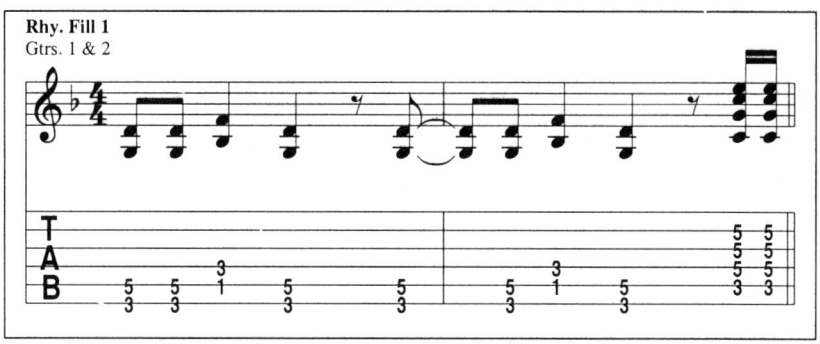

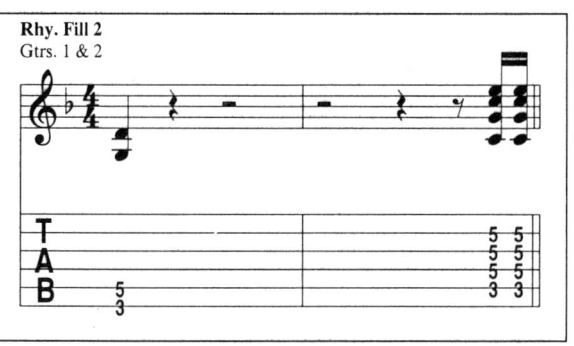

33

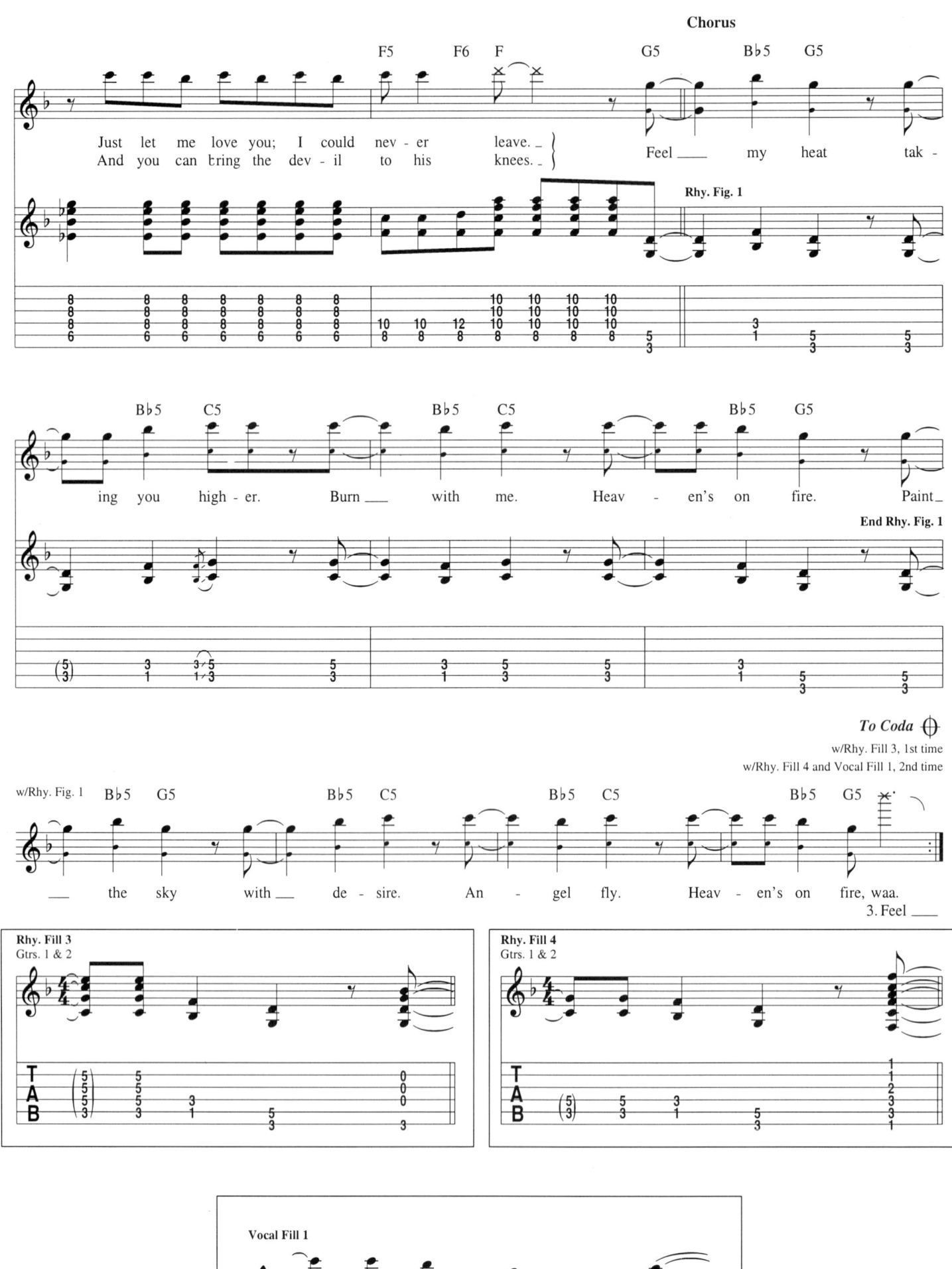

Hit Me with Your Best Shot

Words and Music by Eddie Schwartz

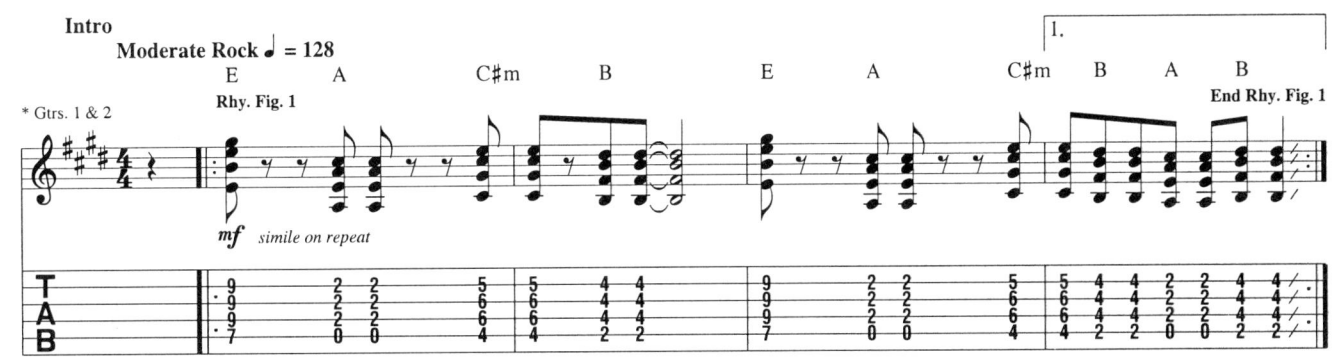

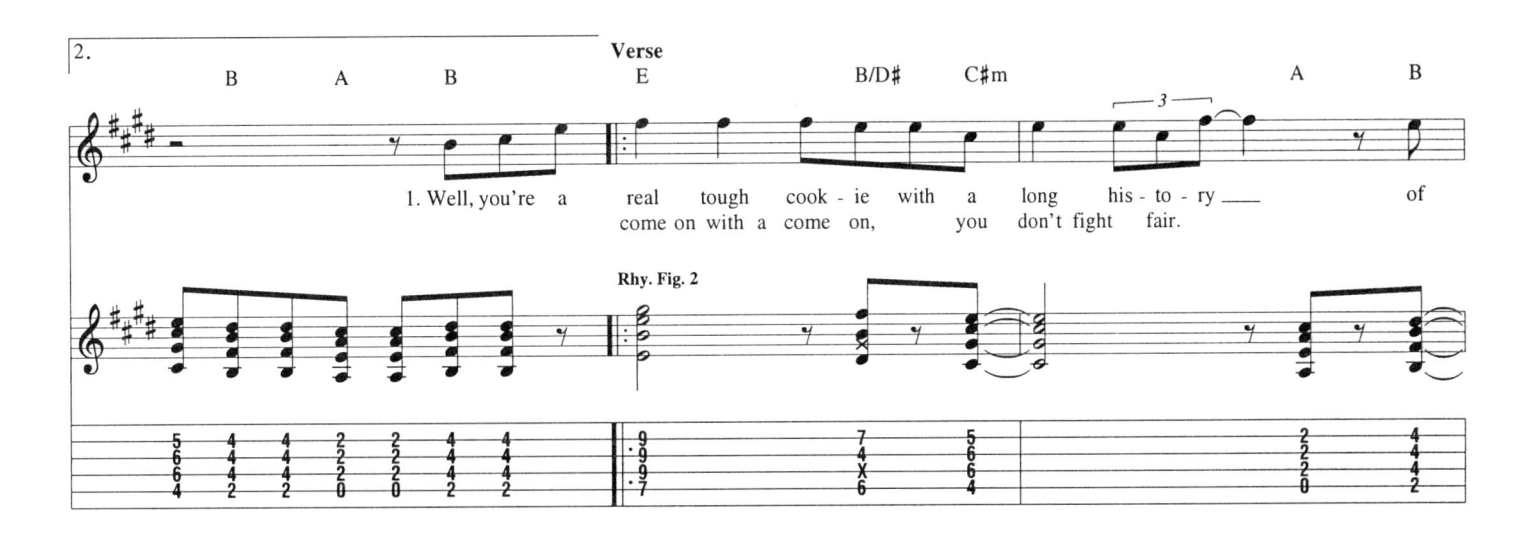

how you do it. Put up your dukes, let's get down to it.
in vain. I'll get right back on my feet a - gain.
End Rhy. Fig. 2
*P.M.
*grad. release
Chorus
Gtrs. 1 & 2: w/ Rhy. Fig. 1, 2 times, simile
E A C♯m B E A C♯m B A B
Hit me with your best shot. Why don't you hit me with your best shot?
E A C♯m B E A C♯m B A B B A B
1. 2.
Hit me with your best shot. Fire a - way. 2. You
Guitar Solo
Gtrs. 1 & 2: w/ Rhy. Fig. 2
E B/D♯ C♯m A B
Gtr. 3 (dist.)
f
slight P.M.
Gtr. 1: w/ Fill 1
E B/D♯ C♯m A B
P.M.
semi-harm.
full
Gtrs. 1 & 2: w/ Rhy. Fig. 1, 2 times, simile
E A C♯m
B E A C♯m B A B E A C♯m
full

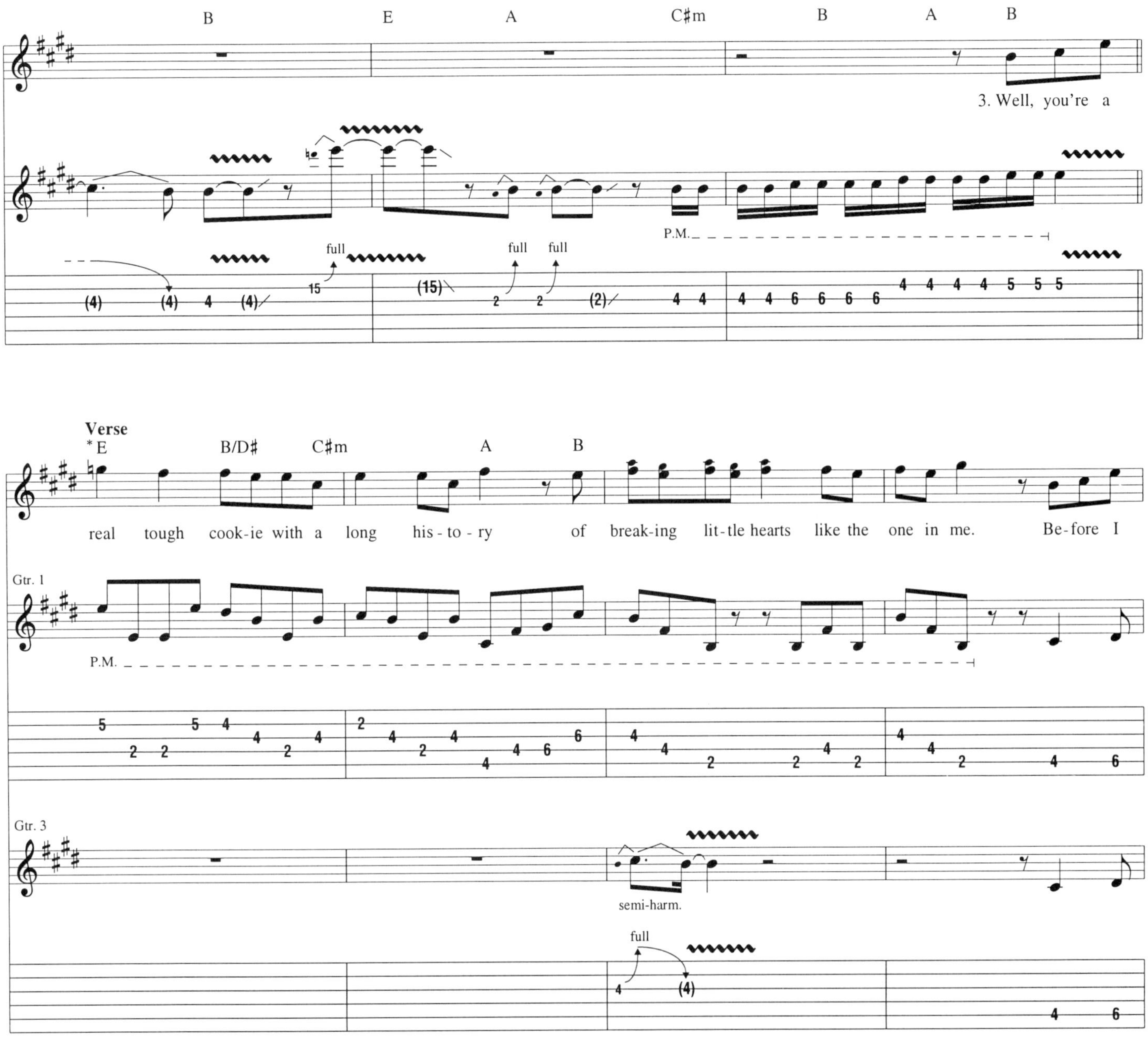

* Chord symbols reflect implied tonality.

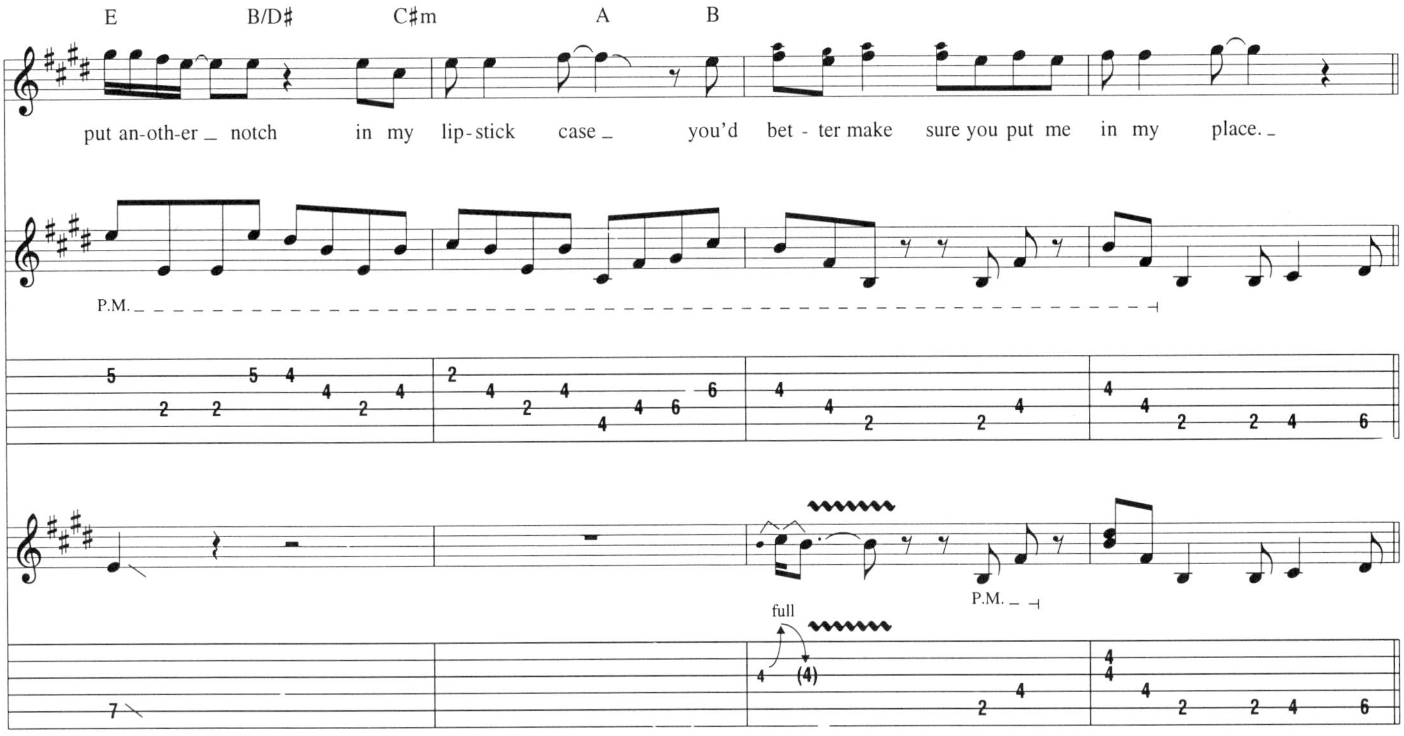

Chorus
Gtrs. 1 & 3: w/ Rhy. Fig. 1, 2 times, simile
Gtr. 2: w/ Fill 2, 1st time
E A C♯m B E A C♯m B A B
Hit me with your best shot. Come on, hit me with your best shot.
E A C♯m B
1.
E A C♯m B A B
Hit me with your best shot. Fire a - way.
2.
E A C♯m B A B
Outro
E
1., 2.
A C♯m B A B E
Gtrs. 1 & 3
3.
B A B
Gtr. 1
Freely
E
E7
1/4 1/4 1/4
let ring
Gtr. 3
Fill 2
Gtr. 2
play 7 times

Money for Nothing

Words and Music by Mark Knopfler and Sting

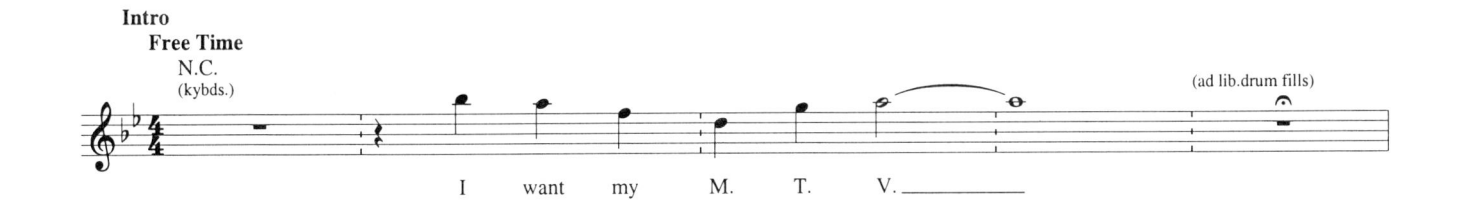

Intro
Free Time
N.C. (kybds.)

I want my M. T. V. _____ (ad lib. drum fills)

Moderate Rock ♩ = 135

*G5   B♭5 C5 G5

Gtr. 1 (dist.)
mf w/ fingers
Harm.

Chord symbols reflect implied tonality.

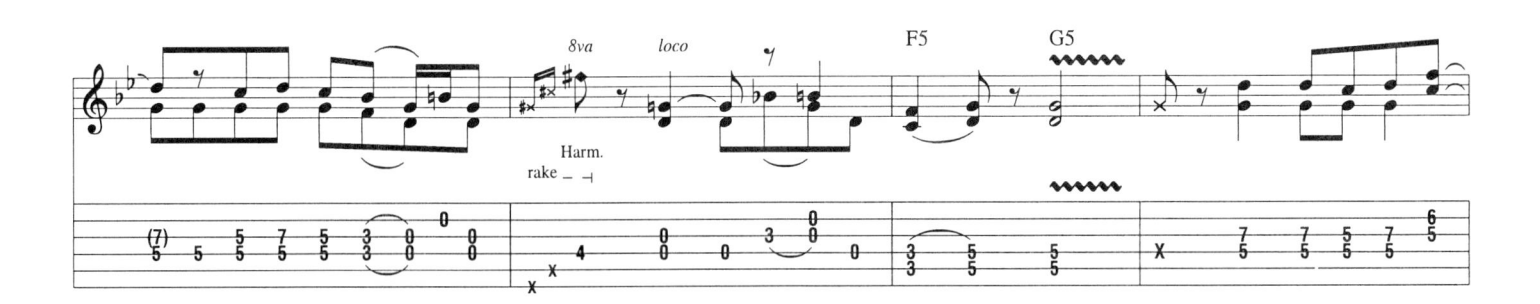

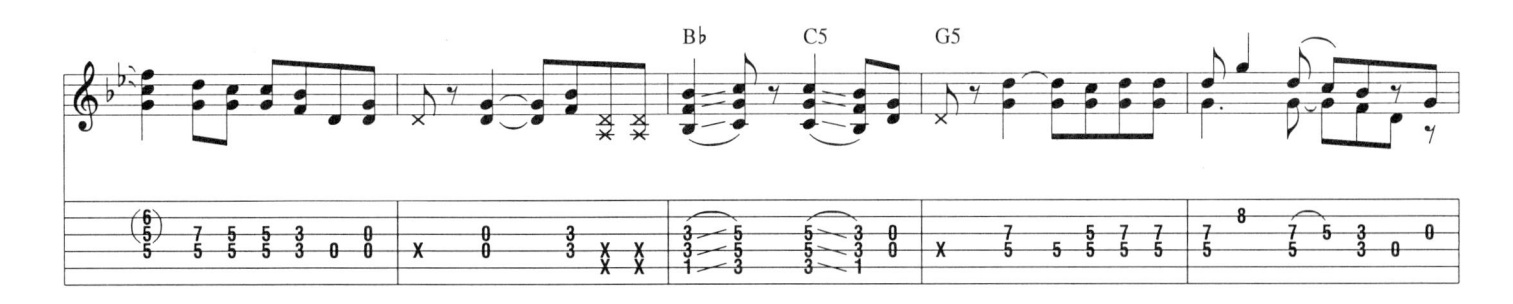

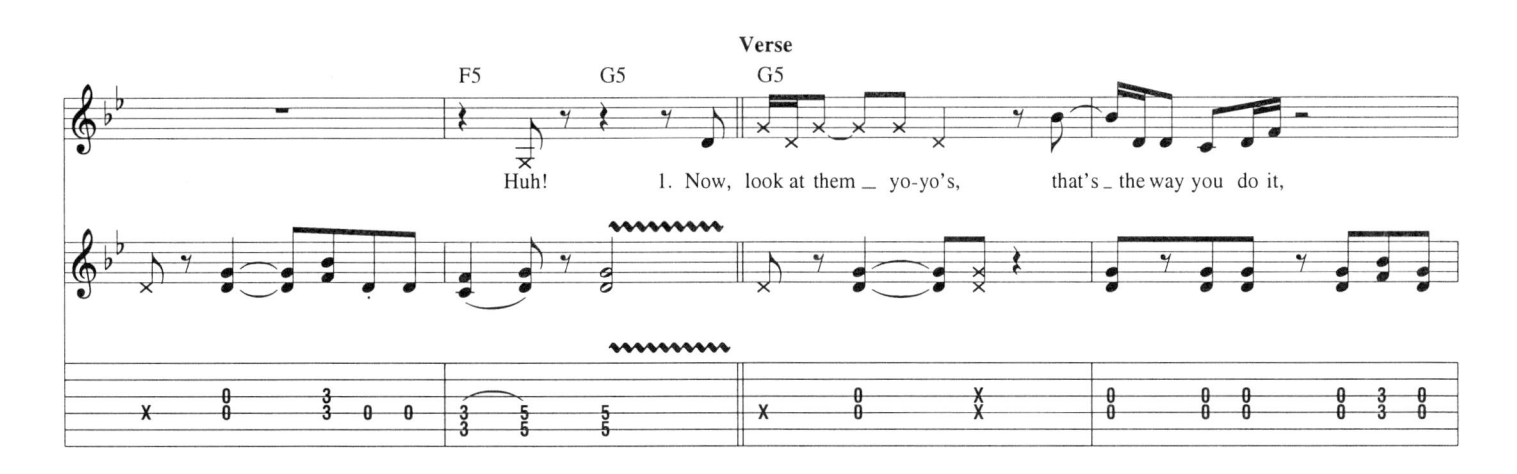

8va loco   F5   G5
Harm.
rake

B♭   C5   G5

Verse
F5   G5   G5

Huh!   1. Now, look at them _ yo-yo's,   that's _ the way you do it,

---

Copyright © 1985 Chariscourt Ltd. and Gordon M. Sumner
Gordon M. Sumner Published by Magnetic Publishing Ltd. (PRS)
Represented by Blue Turtle Music and Administered by Almo Music Corp. (ASCAP) in the U.S. and Canada
International Copyright Secured   All Rights Reserved

B♭5 C5 G5
you play the gui - tar on the M. T. V. __ That ain't ____ work - in', that's __ the way you do it,
F5 G5
mon - ey for noth - in' and your chicks for free. ______ Now, that ain't work - in', that's _
B♭5 C5
__ the way you do it, lem - me tell ya them __ guys ain't dumb. __ You
G5 F5 G5
may - be get a blis - ter on your lit - tle fin - ger, may - be get a blis - ter on your _ thumb. _
8va
loco
Harm.

pitch : D

43

G5
F5
G5
Huh!
Gtr. 2
Gtr. 1
Chorus
Eb5
Bb5
Eb5
F5
(Got-ta in - stall mi-cro-wave ov-ens, cus-tom kitch-en de - liv - er - ies.
G5
C5
D5
We got - ta move these re-frig-er-a-tors.
We got-ta move these re-frig-er-a-tors, we got-ta move these col-or T V's.

45

Lyrics:

have some fun. And he's up there. What's that? Hawaiian noises? He's bangin' on the bongos like a chimpanzee. Oh, that ain't workin', that's the way you do it, get your money for nothin', get your chicks for free.
(That's the way you do it, money for nothin', get your chicks for free.)

Chorus
We gotta install microwave ovens, custom kitchen deliveries.

G5
C5
We got-ta move these re-frig-er-a-tors, we got-ta move these
(We got-ta move these re-frig-er-a-tors.)
D5
E5
Interlude
G5
co-lor T V's.
Gtr. 2
Gtr. 1
B♭5
C5
G5
Ow!
1/2

Outro
F5 G5
Lis-ten here. Now, that ain't work-ing, that's the way you do it,
you play the gui - tar on the M. T. V.
B♭5 C5 G5
That ain't work - in, that's

w/ Lead Voc. ad lib., till fade
F5
G5
_ the way you do it, mon-ey for noth-in' and your chicks for free. _ Mon-ey for noth-in',
8va
loco
Harm.
Bb5
C5
G5
and your chicks for free. _ Get your mon-ey for noth - in'
full
full
full
hold bend
8va
loco
Harm.

50

Oh, Pretty Woman

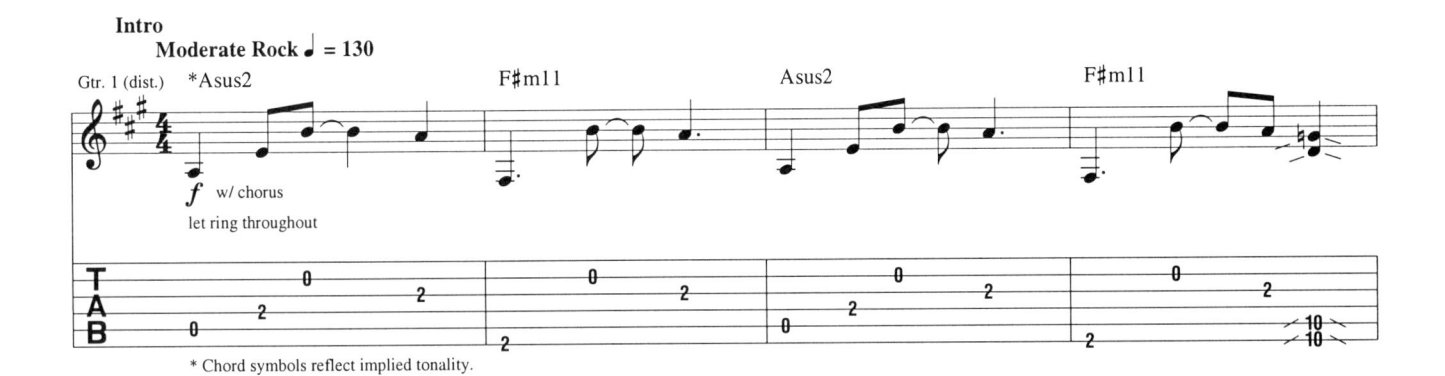

Words and Music by Roy Orbison and Bill Dees

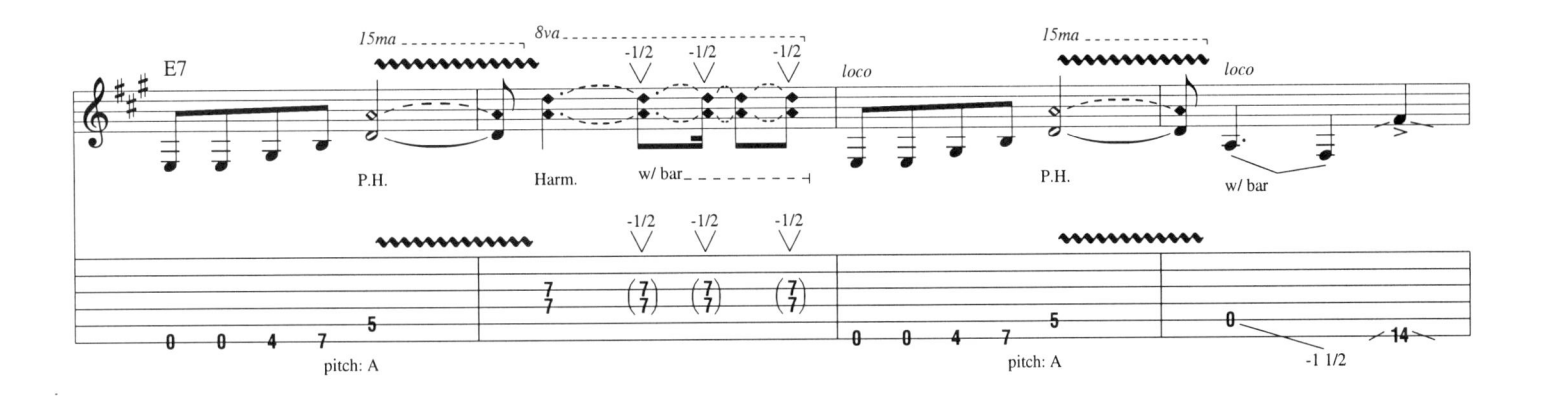

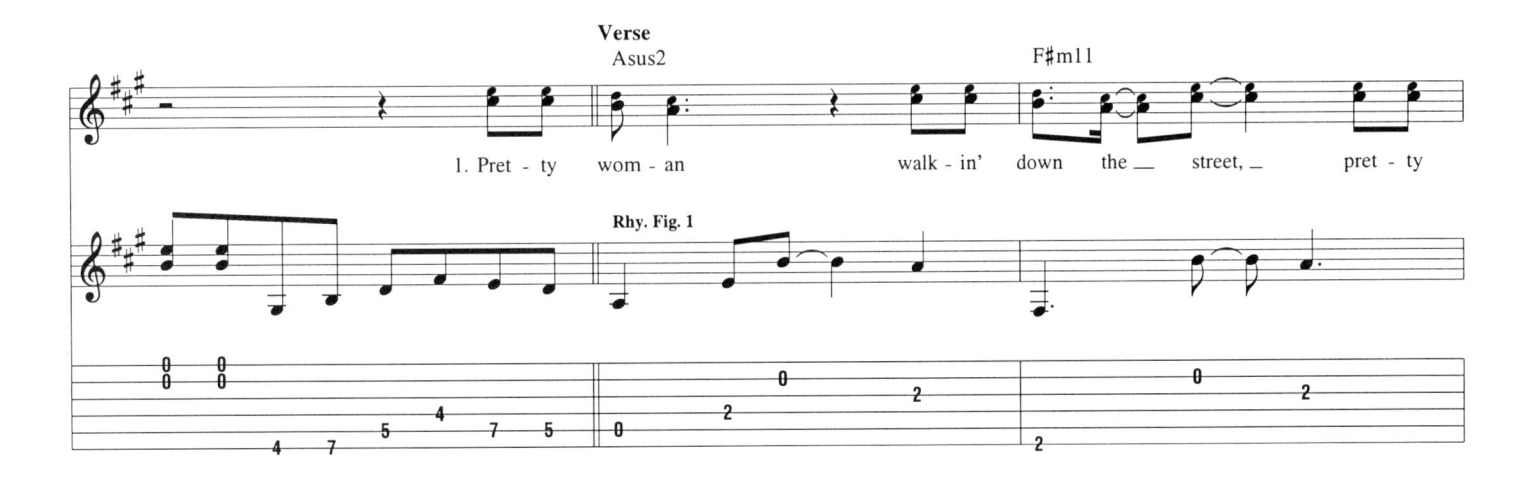

Tune Down 1/2 Step:
① = E♭ ④ = D♭
② = B♭ ⑤ = A♭
③ = G♭ ⑥ = E♭

*Chord symbols reflect implied tonality.

52

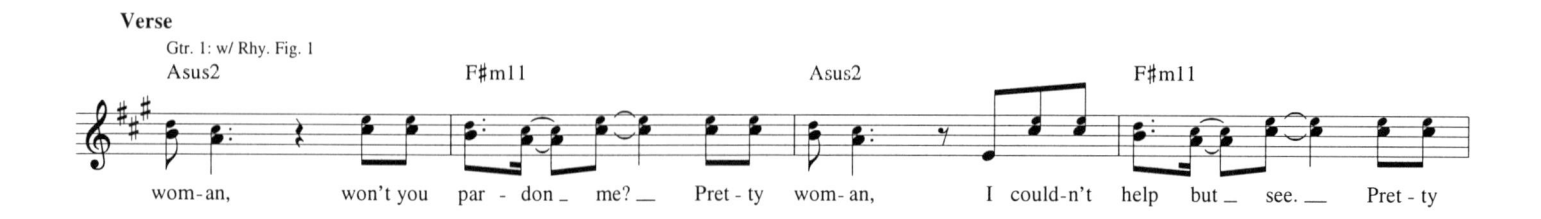

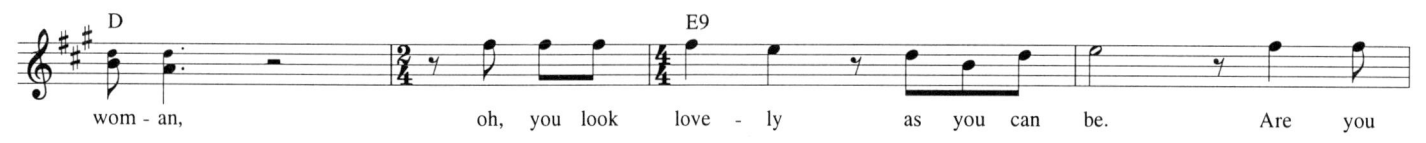

Interlude
E7
lone - ly just like me?
Gtr. 1
tr
P.M.
Bridge
Dm G5 Cadd9 G/B Asus2 Am Asus4
Pret-ty wom - an, stop a - while.
Pret-ty wom - an, talk a - while.
Gtr. 1
Gtr. 2 (clean)
mf
let ring throughout

Dm
G5
Cadd9
C
Pret-ty wom - an, give your smile _ to me.
Dm
G5
C
G/B
Asus2
Asus4
Pret-ty wom - an, yeah, yeah, yeah.
Pret-ty wom - an, look my way.

Pret-ty wom - an, say you'll stay with me 'cause I need you, need you to - night.

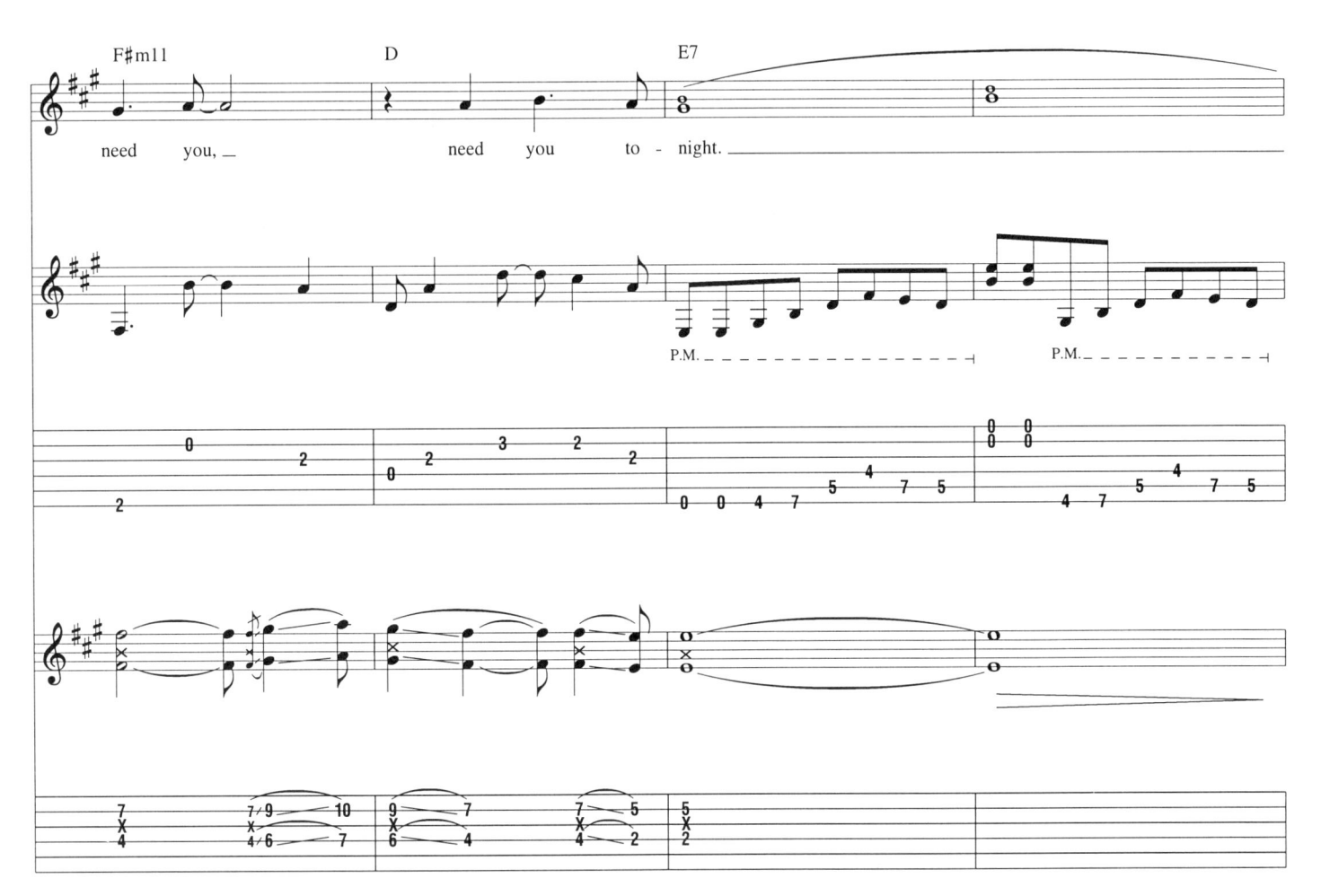

Gtr. 2 tacet
3. Pret - ty
Gtr. 1
P.M.
Verse
Gtr. 1: w/ Rhy. Fig. 1
Asus2
F♯m11
Asus2
F♯m11
wom - an, don't walk on by. Pret - ty wom - an, don't make me cry. Pret - ty
D
E9
wom - an, don't walk a - way, hey.
O. K. If that's the way it must be, O.
Gtr. 1
K. I guess I'll go on home. It's late.

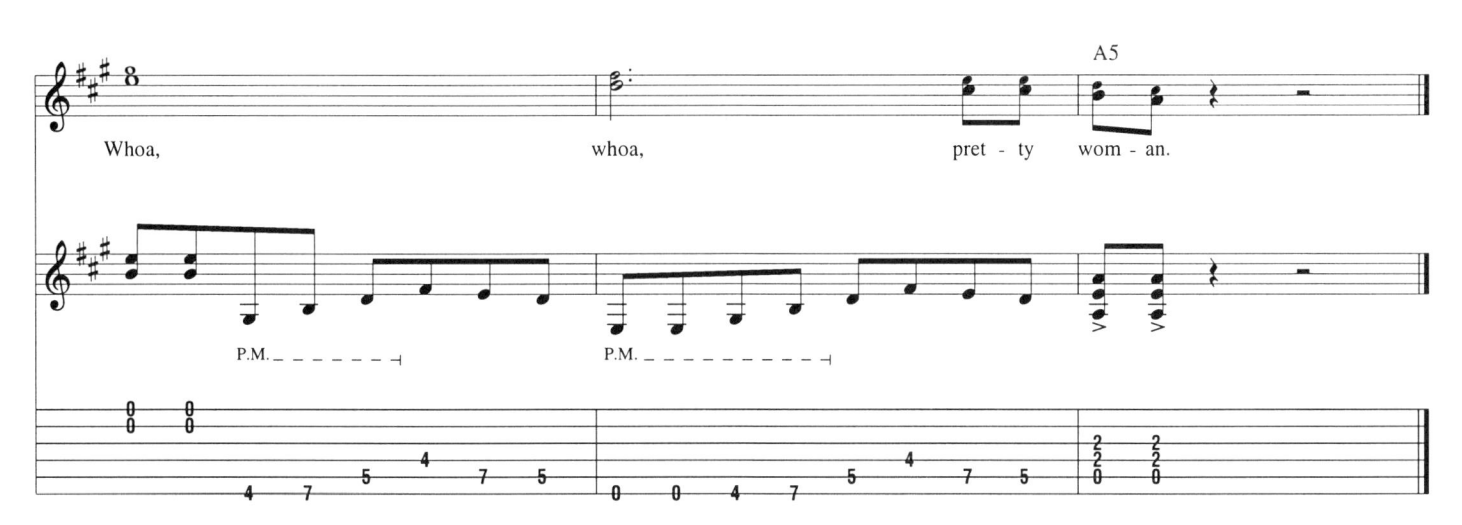

There'll be to-mor-row night. But wait! What do I see?

She's walk-ing back to me.

Outro

Whoa, whoa, pret-ty wom-an.

Pretending

Words and Music by Jerry Williams

*Key signature denotes E Dorian.
**Chord symbols reflect overall tonality.

Copyright © 1985 by Careers-BMG Music Publishing, Inc., Hamstein Music and Urge Music
International Copyright Secured   All Rights Reserved

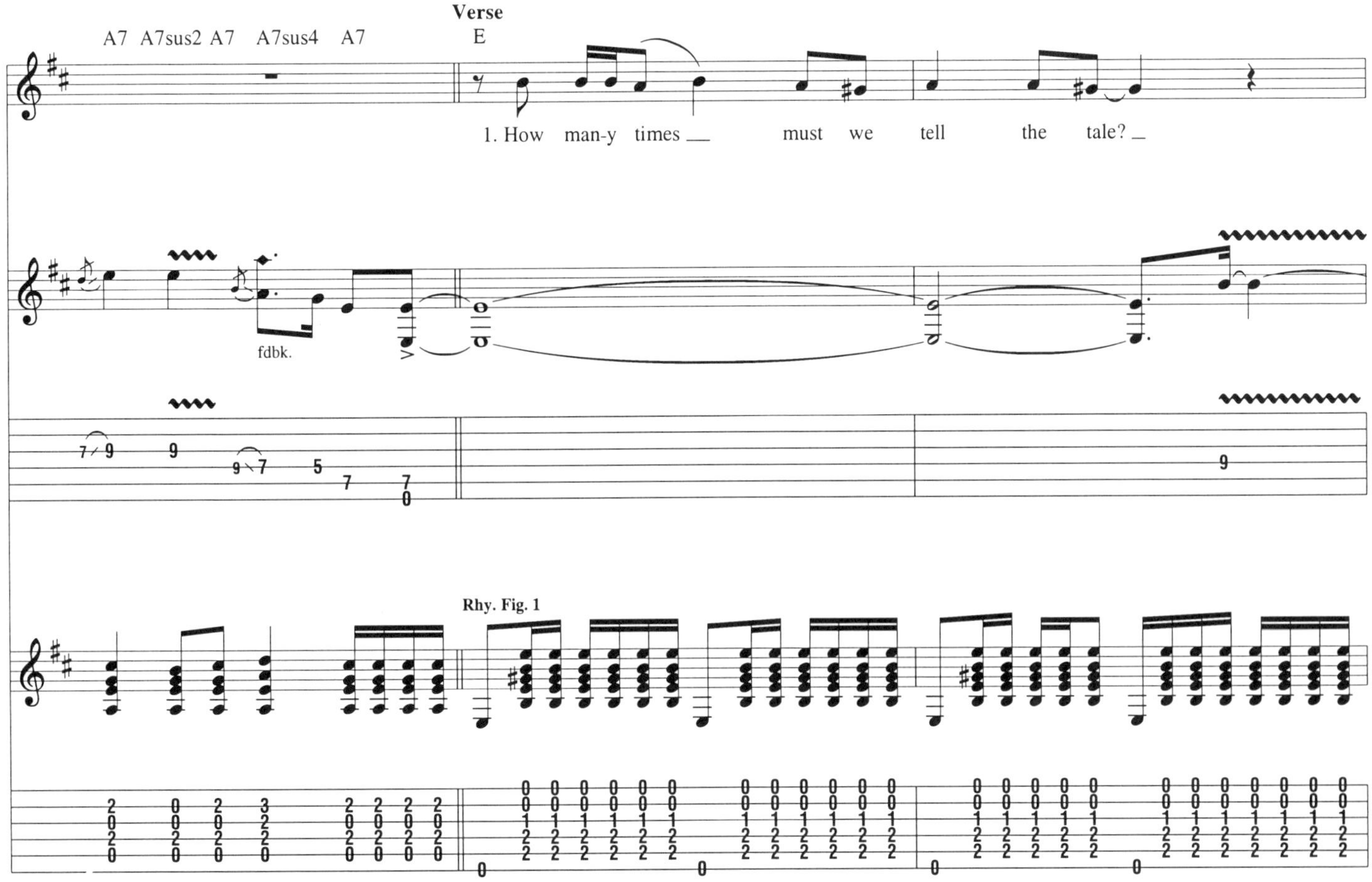
A7 A7sus2 A7 A7sus4 A7
Verse
E
1. How man-y times must we tell the tale?
fdbk.
Rhy. Fig. 1

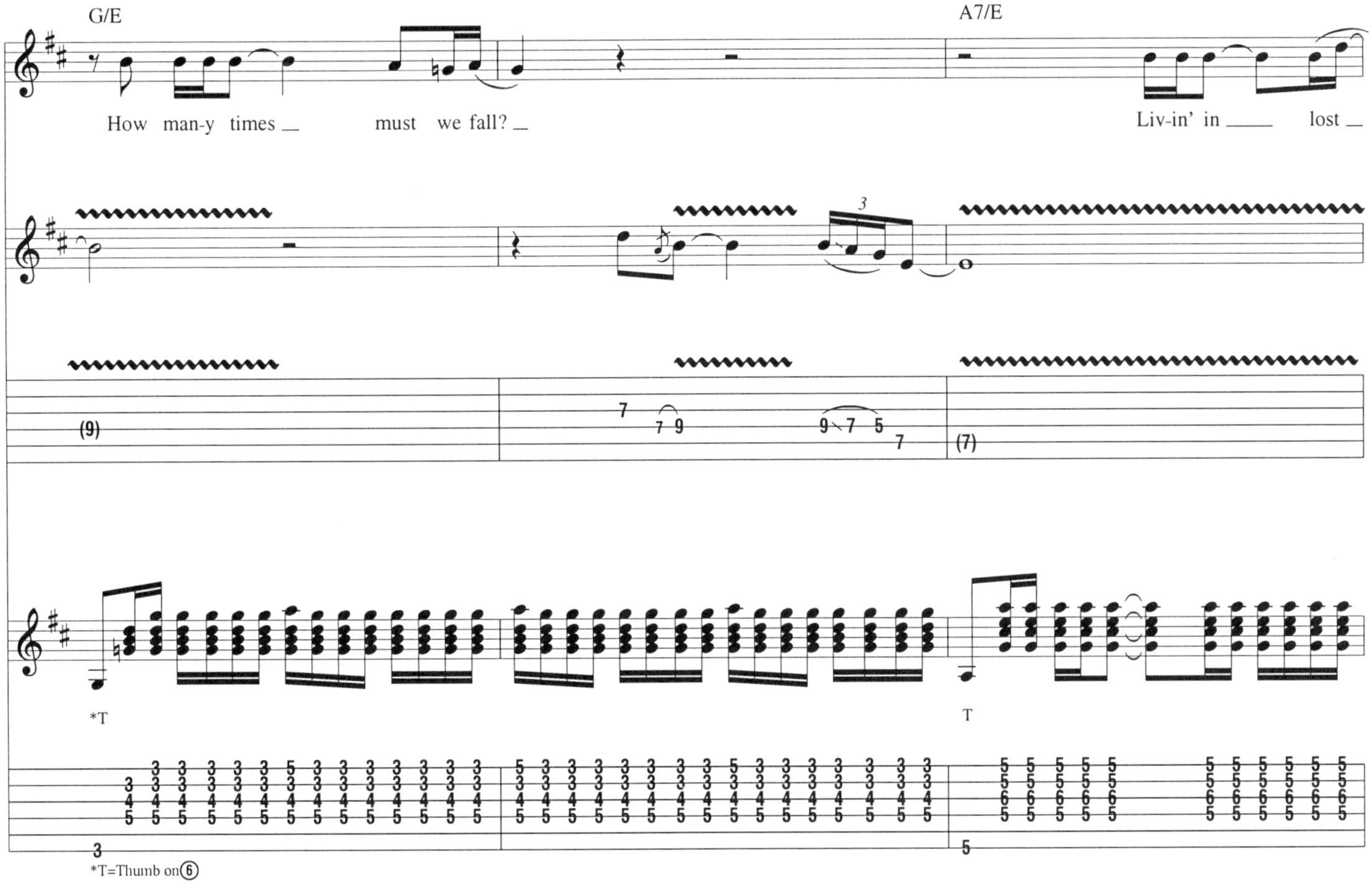
G/E
A7/E
How man-y times must we fall?
Liv-in' in lost
*T
T
*T=Thumb on ⑥

60

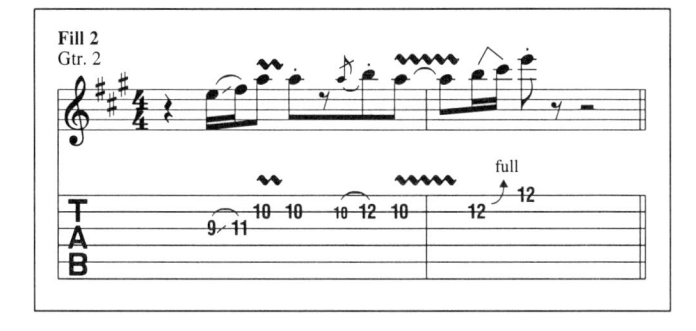

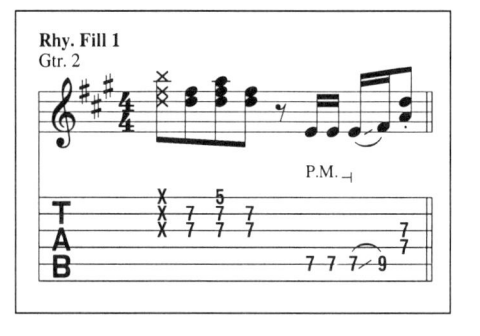

% Chorus

That's when she said she was pretending, just like she knew the plan.

That's when I knew she was pretending, pretending to understand. Pre-

Gtr. 2: w/ Riff A, 2 times
E7
tend - ing, pre - tend - ing, pre -
Gtr. 1
full
full
A7
E7
tend - ing, pre - tend - ing.
full
full
Verse
Gtr. 2: w/ Rhy. Fig. 1
E
G/E
3.Sa-tis - fied, but lost in love, sit - u - a - tions change.
Harm.
D.S. al Coda
Gtr. 2: w/ Fill 1
A7
A7sus4
A7
E
N.C.
You're nev-er who you used to think you are, how strange.

Coda
Gtr. 2: w/ Riff A, 2 times
E7
tend - ing,
pre - tend - ing,
Gtr. 1
full
A7
pre - tend - ing,
pre -
1/4
E7
tend - ing.
(Pre - tend - ing, pre - tend - ing.)
Guitar Solo
Gtr. 2: w/ Rhy. Fig. 1
E
G/E
hold bend
even release
A7
A7sus4
A7
E
1/2
1 1/2
Verse
Gtr. 2: w/ Rhy. Fig. 1, 1st 7 meas.
E
4. I get lost in

G/E
A7
al - i - bis,
sad - ness can't
pre - vail.
Ev-'ry bod-y
fdbk.
Chorus
Gtr. 2: w/ Fill 1
Gtr. 2: w/ Rhy. Fig. 2, simile
A7sus4
A7
E
N.C.
A
E
knows strong love can't
fail.
Don't be pre
tend - ing
1/4
D
A
E
D
A
E
a-bout how you feel.
Don't be pre - tend - ing
D
A
E
1.
D
2.
D
your love is
real.
Don't be pre -
Pre -

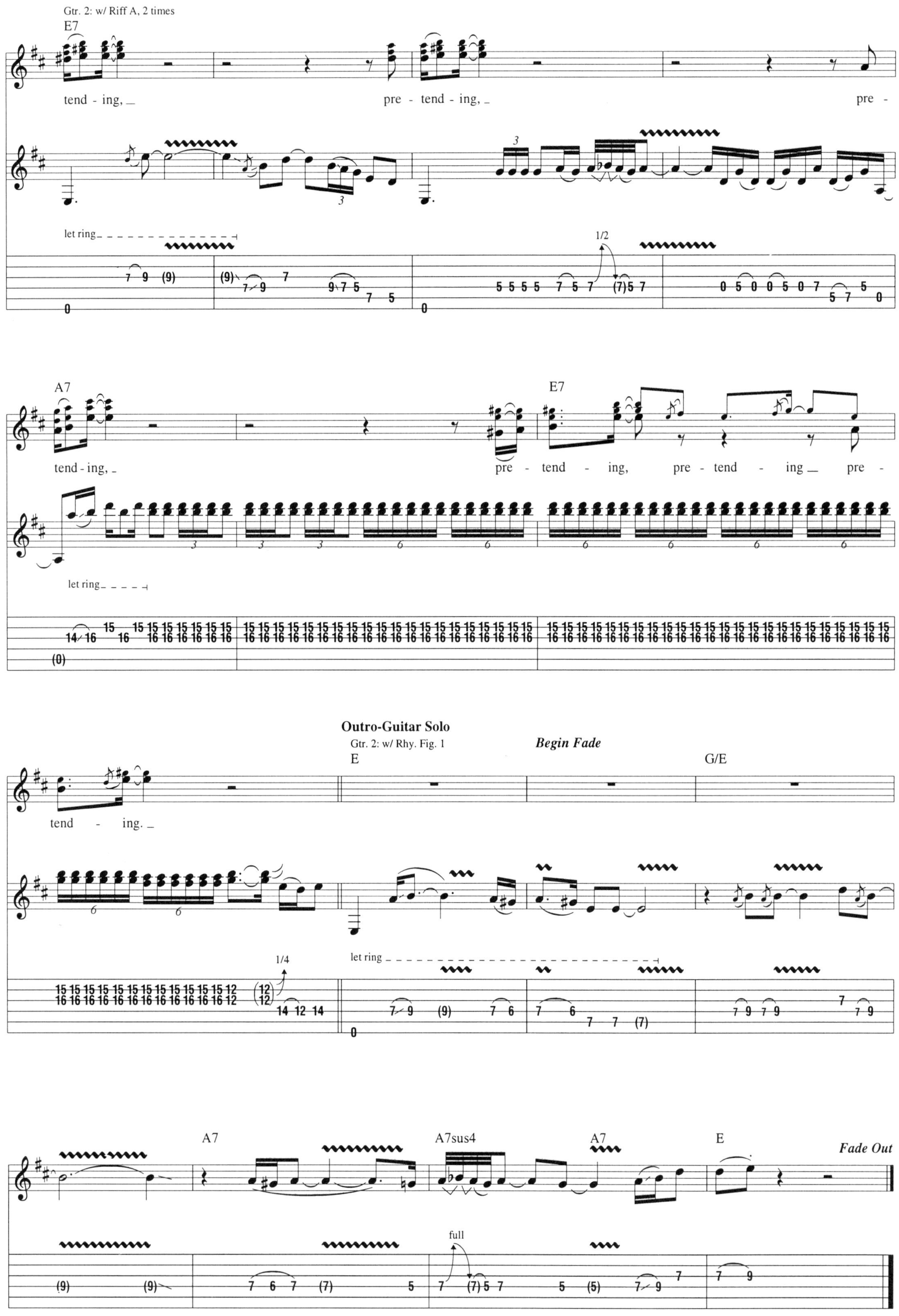
Gtr. 2: w/ Riff A, 2 times
E7
tend - ing, pre - tend - ing, pre -
let ring
1/2
A7
E7
tend - ing, pre - tend - ing, pre - tend - ing pre -
let ring
Outro-Guitar Solo
Gtr. 2: w/ Rhy. Fig. 1
Begin Fade
E
G/E
tend - ing.
1/4
let ring
A7
A7sus4
A7
E
Fade Out
full

Pride and Joy

By Stevie Ray Vaughan

Tune Down 1/2 Step:
① = E♭ ④ = D♭
② = B♭ ⑤ = A♭
③ = G♭ ⑥ = E♭

Verse
B7
E
1. Well, you've heard a - bout lov - in' giv - in' sight __ to the blind. __
mf
sim.
1/2
let ring
* Mute w/ palm of pick hand.
My ba - by's lov - in' 'cause the sun __ to shine. _ An' she's my sweet _ lit - tle thang, __
A7
f
she('s) my pride and joy. __
E
She('s) _ my
1/4
P.M.
B7
A7
E
sweet lit - tle ba - by, I'm __ her __ lit - tle lov - er boy. __
let ring
rake

Verse
B7
E
2. Yeah, I love my ba - by, my heart and ___ soul. ___
mf
A7
Love like ours ___ ah, won't nev - er grow _ old. ___ She('s) my sweet ___ lit - tle thang, ___
f
1/4
E
she('s) my pride and joy. ___ She('s) ___ my
mf
P.M.
B7
A7
E
sweet lit - tle ba - by, I'm ___ her ___ lit - tle lov - er boy. ___
f

Verse
B7
E N.C.
E N.C.
3. Yeah, I love my la-dy to be long and lean.
full
full
E N.C.
E
A7
You mess with her, you'll see a man get-tin' mean.
She('s) my sweet lit-tle thang,
E
she('s) my pride and joy.
She('s) my
let ring
1/4
1/2
1/2
1/4

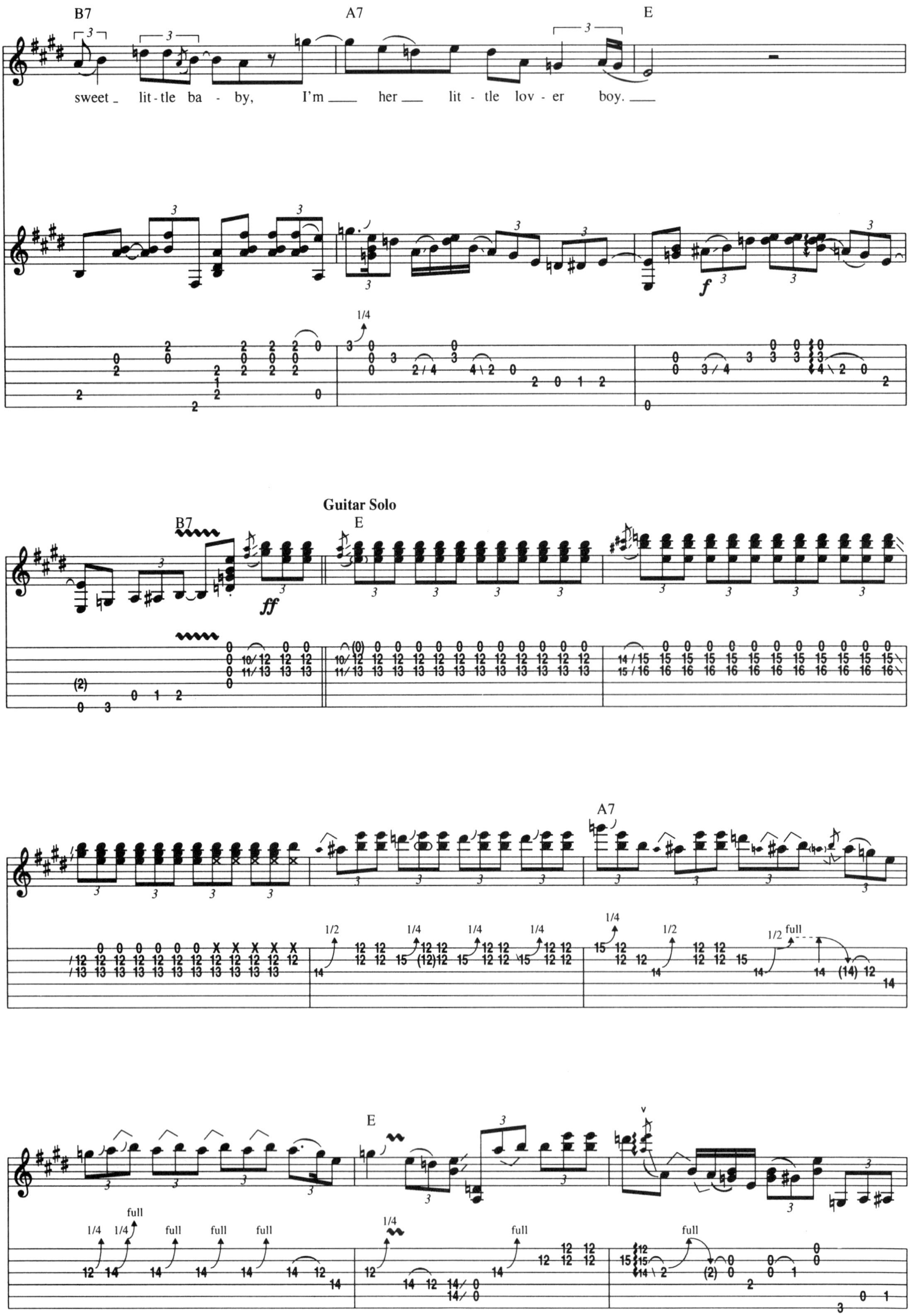
B7
A7
E
sweet _ lit-tle ba - by, I'm ___ her ___ lit - tle lov - er boy. ___
Guitar Solo
B7
E
A7
E

4. Well, I love my ba-by like the fin-est w, wine.

E N.C.
Asus4
A7
Stick with her __ un - til the end of time. _ An' she('s) my sweet __ lit - tle thang, _
mp
f
1/4
E
she('s) my pride and joy. __
She('s) my
mf
B7
A7
E
sweet lit - tle ba - by, I'm ___ her ___ lit - tle lov - er boy. ___
f
Verse
B7
E
5. Yeah, I love my ba - by, my heart and __ soul. _
mf

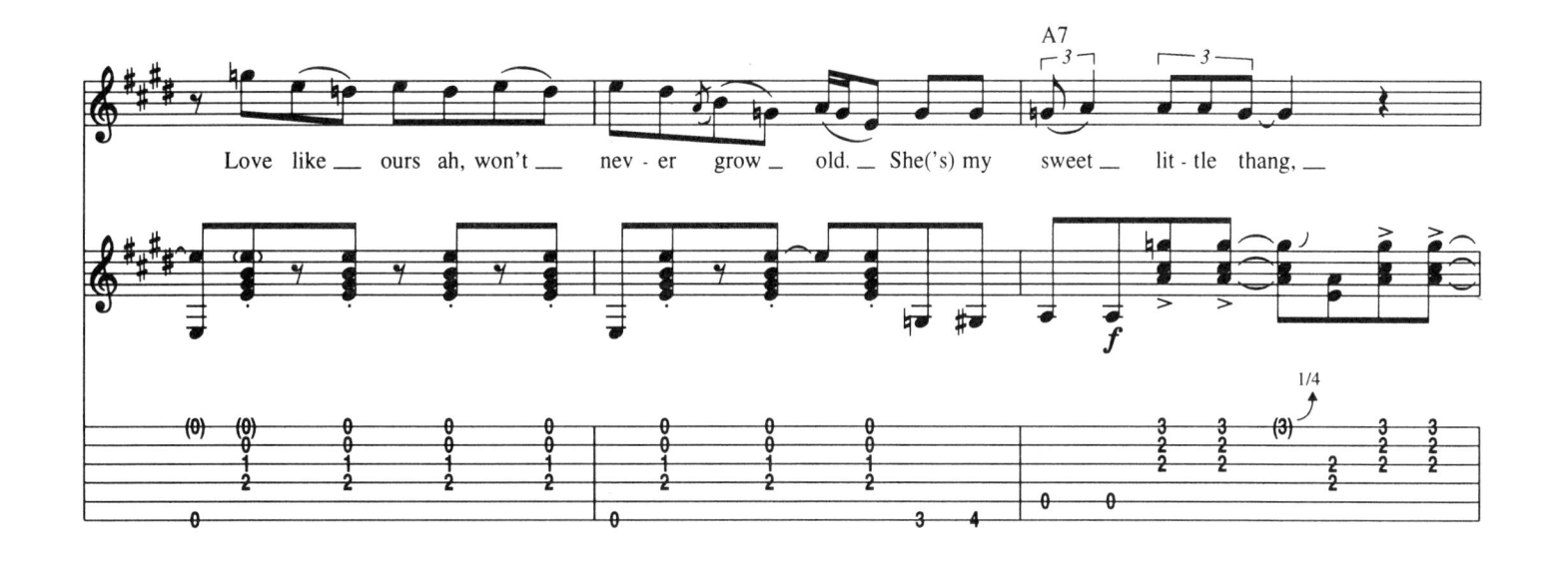

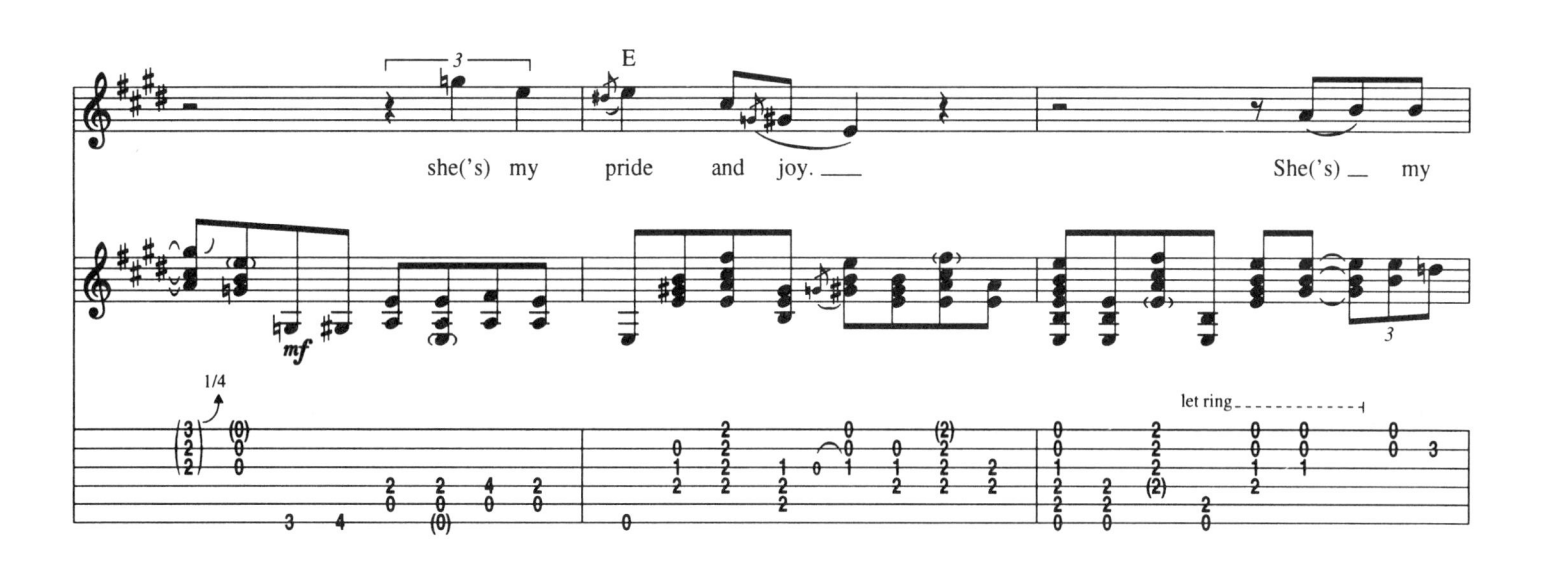

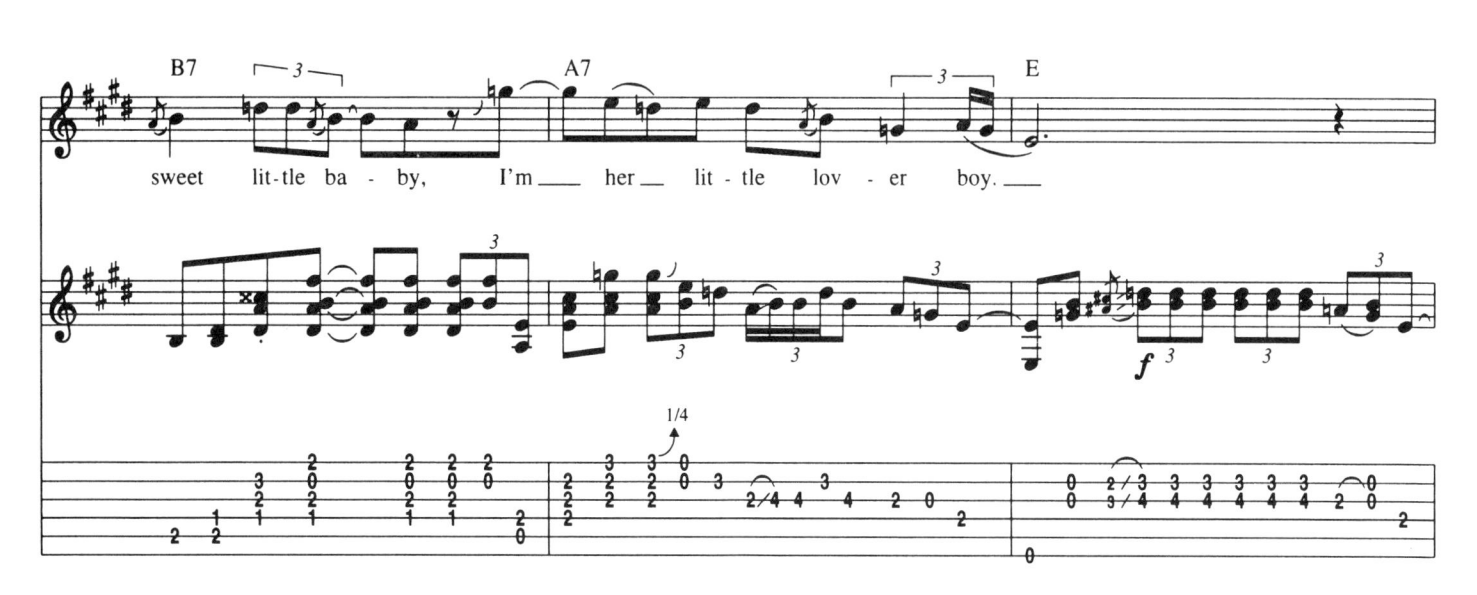

Love like ours ah, won't never grow old. She('s) my sweet little thang,

she('s) my pride and joy. She('s) my

sweet little baby, I'm her little lover boy.

Guitar Solo

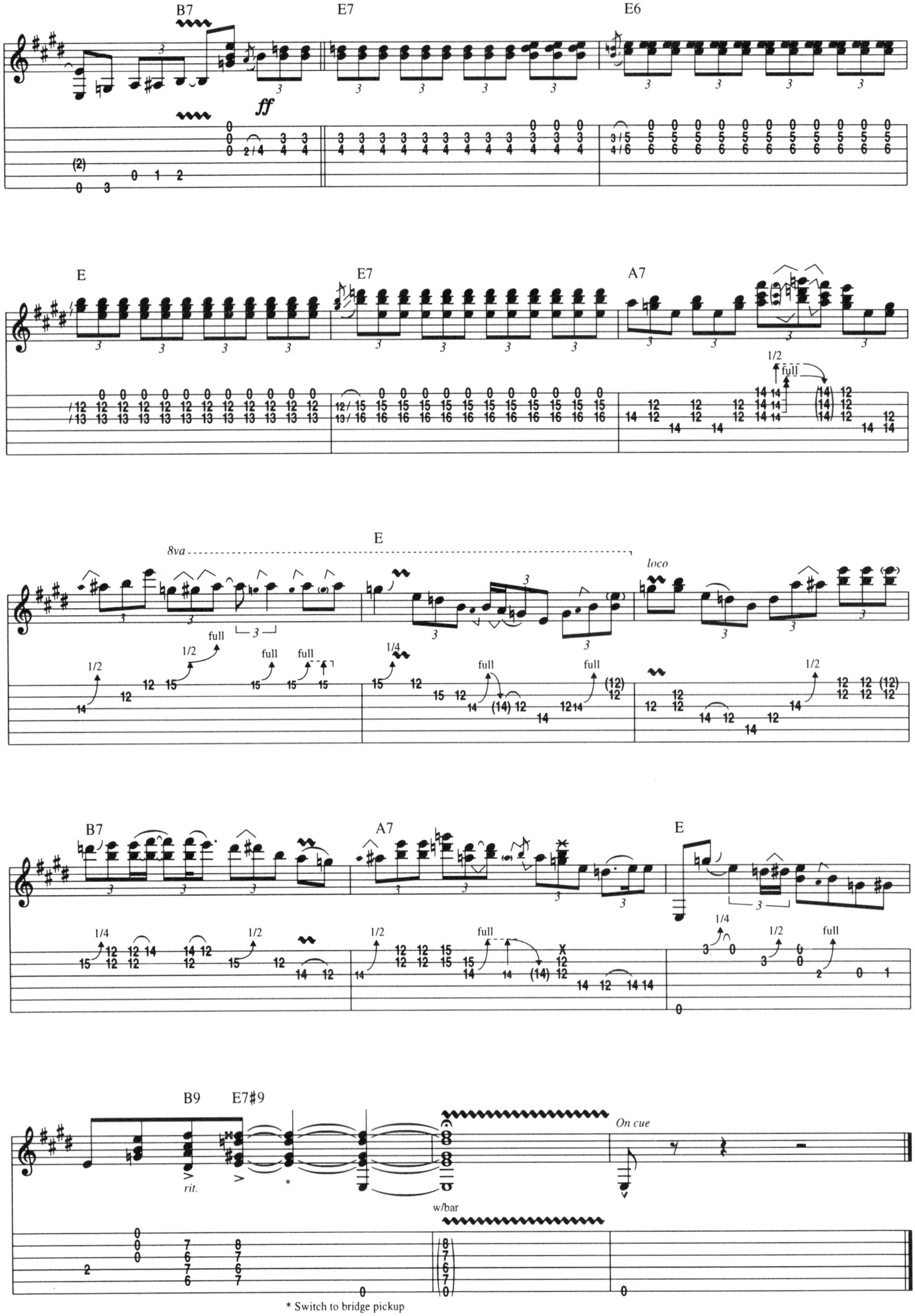

* Switch to bridge pickup

Verse
Gtr. 1: w/ Rhy. Fig. 1, simile
B5 D5 G
Gtr. 1: w/ Rhy. Fig. 1, simile
B5 D5 G
night!
2. Bro - ken bot - tles un - der chil - dren's feet,
) 3. And the bat - tle's just be - gun,
Gtr. 1: w/ Riff A, 1 1/2 times, simile
Bm D G6 Bm D
bod - ies strewn a - cross the dead - end street.
But I won't heed the bat - tle
there's man - y lost, but tell me who has won?
The trench - es dug with - in our
G6 Bm D G6
call.
It puts my back up, puts my back up a - gainst the wall.
hearts,
and moth - ers' chil - dren, broth - ers, sis - ters torn a - part.
Chorus
Gtr. 1: w/ Riff A, simile
Bm D G6 Bm D G6
Sun - day bloo - dy Sun - day.
Sun - day, bloo - dy Sun - day.
1.
N.C.(F) (Em7) (D) (F) (Em7)
Sun - day bloo - dy Sun - day.
Sun - day. bloo - dy Sun - day.
Gtr. 1
Harm.
w/ bar
(D)
Interlude
Gtr. 1: w/ Rhy. Fig. 1, 2 times, simile
2.
D
Oh, let's go!
How long,
*Gtrs. 1 & 2
Harm.
Em D Em
how long must we sing this song? How long, how long?
'Cause to -
(Ah.
* composite arrangement

77

G B5 D5 G
I'll wipe your blood - shot eyes.
- day. Sun - day, blood - y Sun - day.
N.C.(F) (Em7) (D) (F) (Em7) (D)
Sun - day, blood - y Sun - day, ah.
Sun - day, blood - y Sun - day.
Gtr. 1
Harm.
(F) (Em7) (D) (F) (Em7) (D)
Sun - day, blood - y Sun - day, ah. Yeah. let's go!
Sun - day, blood - y Sun - day.
Harm.
Violin Solo
Gtr. 1: w/ Rhy. Fig. 1, 2 times, simile
Verse
Gtr. 1: w/ Rhy. Fig. 1, 8 times, simile
B5 D5 G B5 D5
4. And it's true we are im - mune, when fact is fic - tion and T
G B5 D5 G
V re - al - i - ty. And to - day the mil - lions cry,
Sun - day, blood - y Sun - day.
* Vocals fade in gradually.
B5 D5 G B5 D5
we eat and drink while to - mor - row they die. The real bat - tle yet be - gun,
Sun - day, blood - y Sun - day. Sun - day, blood - y Sun -
G B5 D5 G B5 D5
to claim the vi - t'ry Je - sus won on Sun -
- day. Sun - day, blood - y Sun - day. Sun - day, blood - y Sun -
G B5 D5 G Bm7
Gtr. 1
- day.
- day. Sun - day, blood - y Sun - day.

Sweet Child O' Mine

Words and Music by W. Axl Rose, Slash, Izzy Stradlin', Duff "Rose" McKagan and Steven Adler

Tune Down 1/2 Step:
① = E♭ ④ = G♭
② = A♭ ⑤ = B♭
③ = D♭ ⑥ = E♭

Intro
Medium Rock ♩ = 122

Copyright © 1987 Guns N' Roses Music (ASCAP)
International Copyright Secured All Rights Reserved

79

80

stared _ too _ long, I'll prob-'ly break down and cry. _
pray for the thun- der and the rain _ to qui- et - ly pass _ me by. _

Chorus

Whoa, whoa, _ whoa, _ sweet child o' mine. _

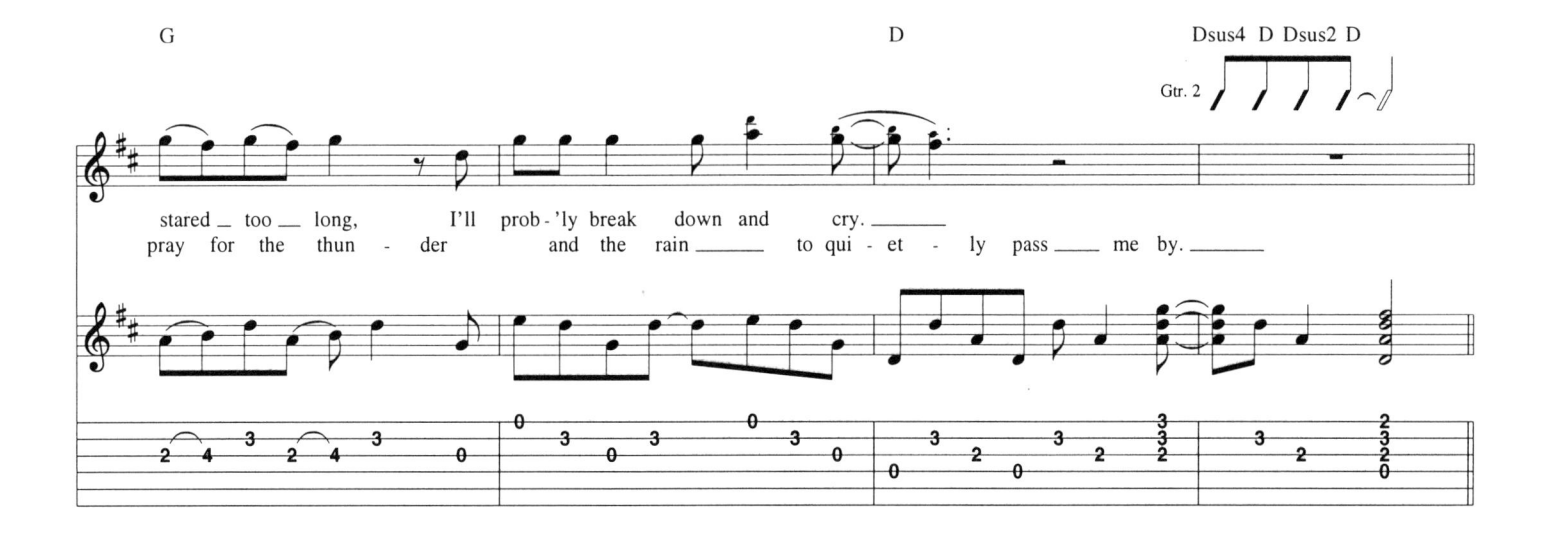

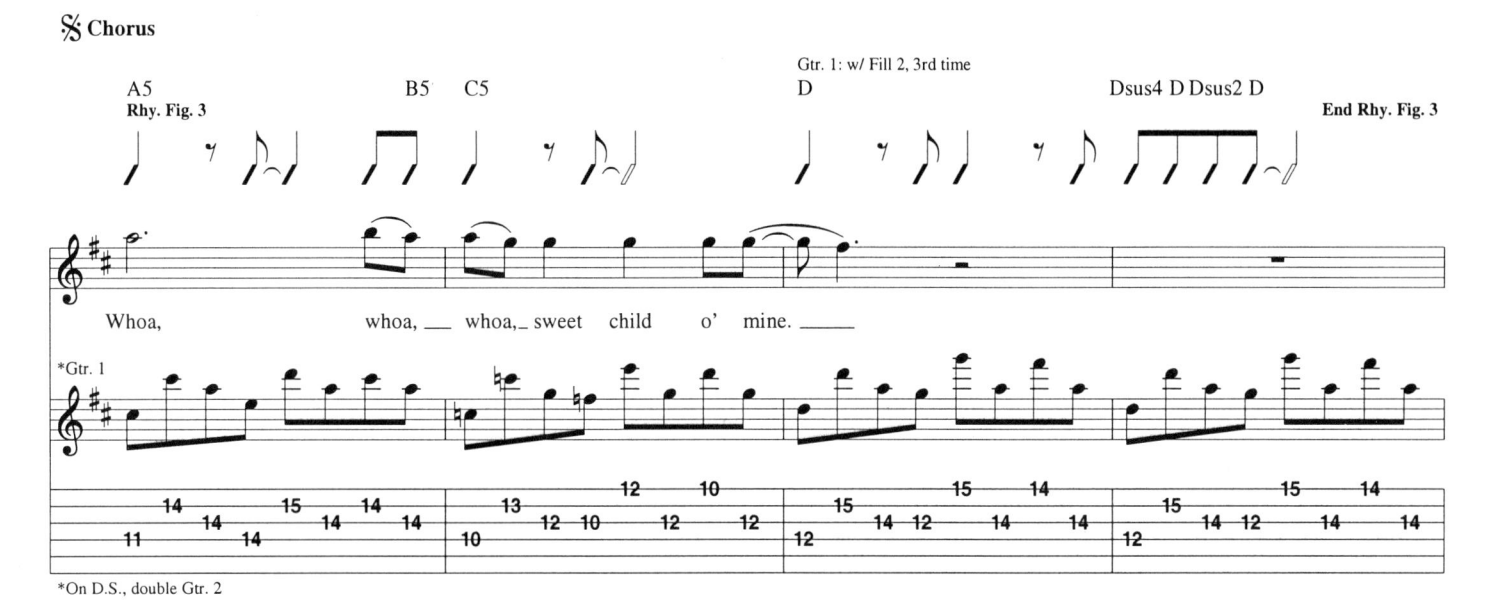

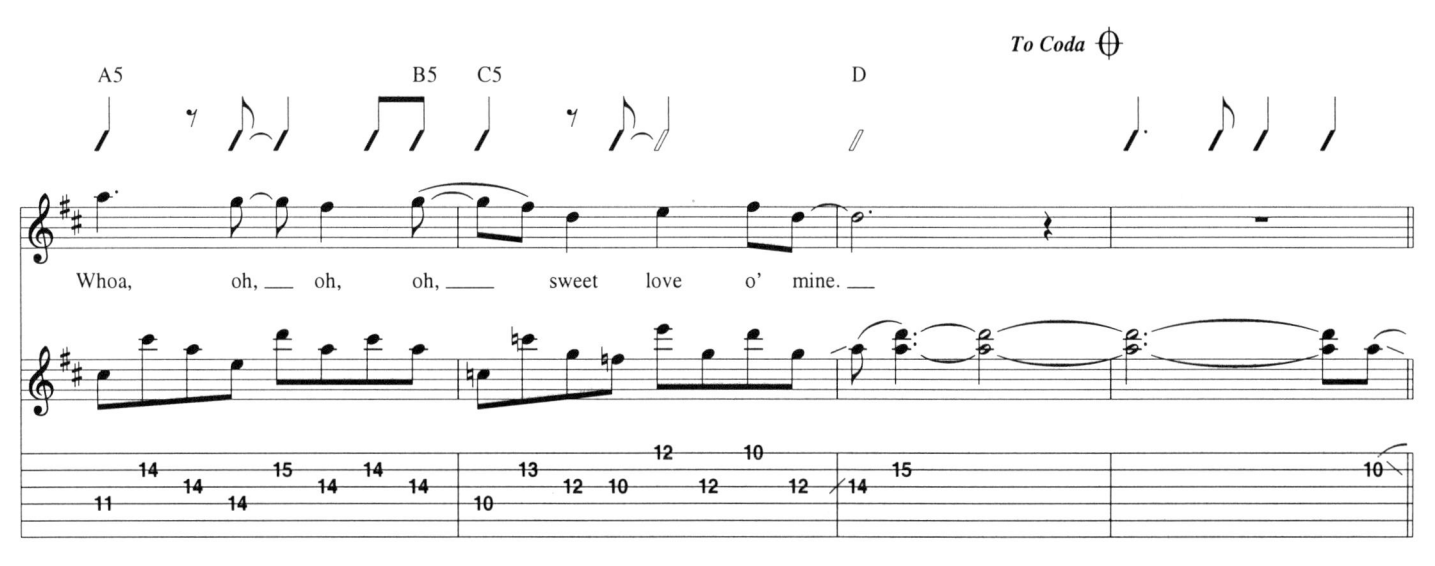

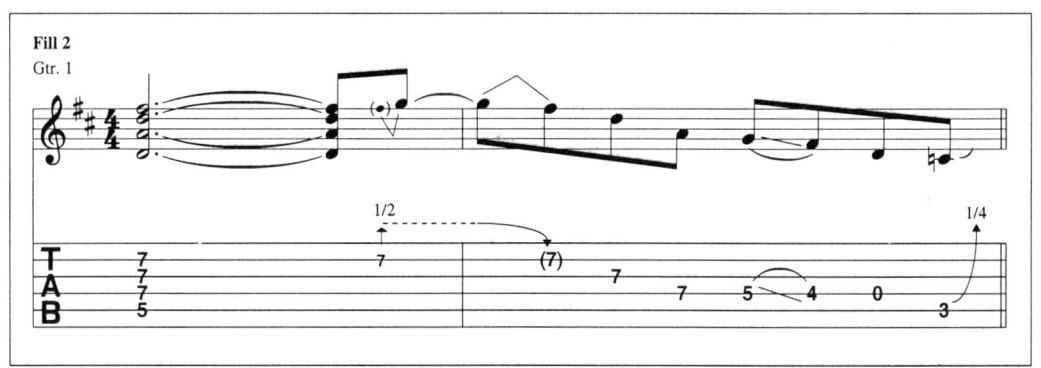

Whoa, oh, _ oh, oh, _ sweet love o' mine. _

Fill 2

Gtr. 2: w/ Rhy. Fig. 1
Gtr. 3: w/ Rhy. Fig. 2
D
C
1.
G
full
full
full
full
D
2.
G
1/2
1/2
hold bend
D
Gtr. 2: w/ Rhy. Fig. 1, first 7 meas.
Gtr. 3: w/ Rhy. Fig. 2
C
1/2
1/2
G
Dsus4 D Dsus2 D
D.S. al Coda
Gtr. 2
8va
full
full
full
full
Coda
D
Gtrs. 1 & 2
Gtrs. 1 & 2: w/ Rhy. Fig. 3, 1 1/2 times
A5
B5 C5
Gtr.1: w/ Fill 2
D
Oh, oh, oh, oh, sweet child o' mine.
A5
B5 C5
D5
Gtrs. 1 & 2
D♯5
Woo, yeah, yeah! Ooh, sweet love o' mine.

Guitar Solo

Em C B7 Am
8va
loco
Gtr. 1
full
full
full
Gtr. 4
Rhy. Fig. 4
End Rhy. Fig. 4
Gtr. 4: w/ Rhy. Fig. 4, 2 times
Em B7 Am Em
8va
loco.
1/2
full
C B7 Am
Gtr. 4: w/ Rhy. Fig. 4, first 3 meas.
Gtr. 5: w/ Fill 3
1/2
full
Fill 3
Gtr. 5
8va
w/ wah - wah
full
TAB

Gtr. 4: w/ Rhy. Fill 1
A5
G F♯
3fr 2fr
Em
Rhy. Fig. 5
E F♯
open 2fr
G5
Gtr. 2
P.M.
8va
Gtr. 5
w/ wah-wah
full
A5
B5
C5
D5
G5
End Rhy. Fig. 5
Gtr. 2: w/ Rhy. Fig. 5, 3 times
loco
1/2
hold bend
E5
1/4
Rhy. Fill 1
Gtr. 4

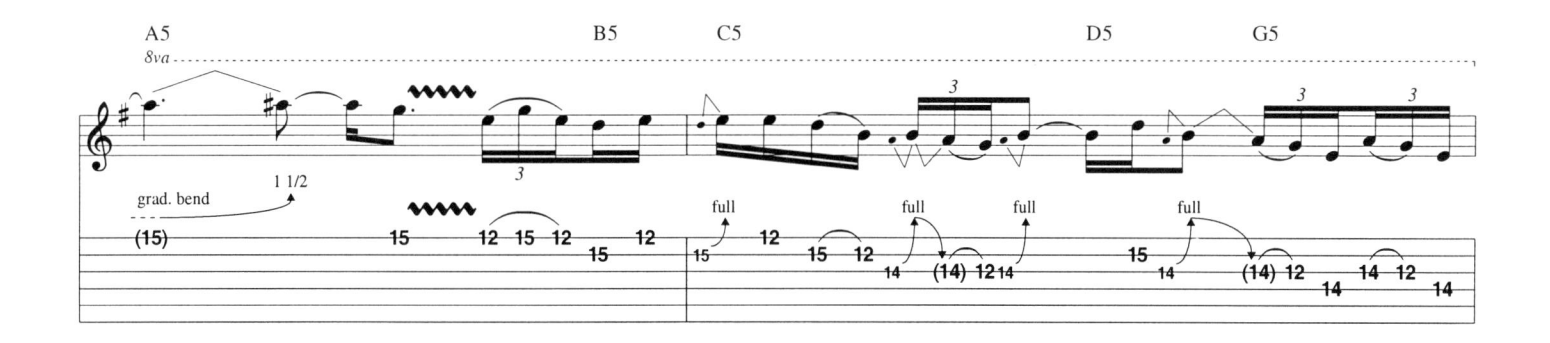

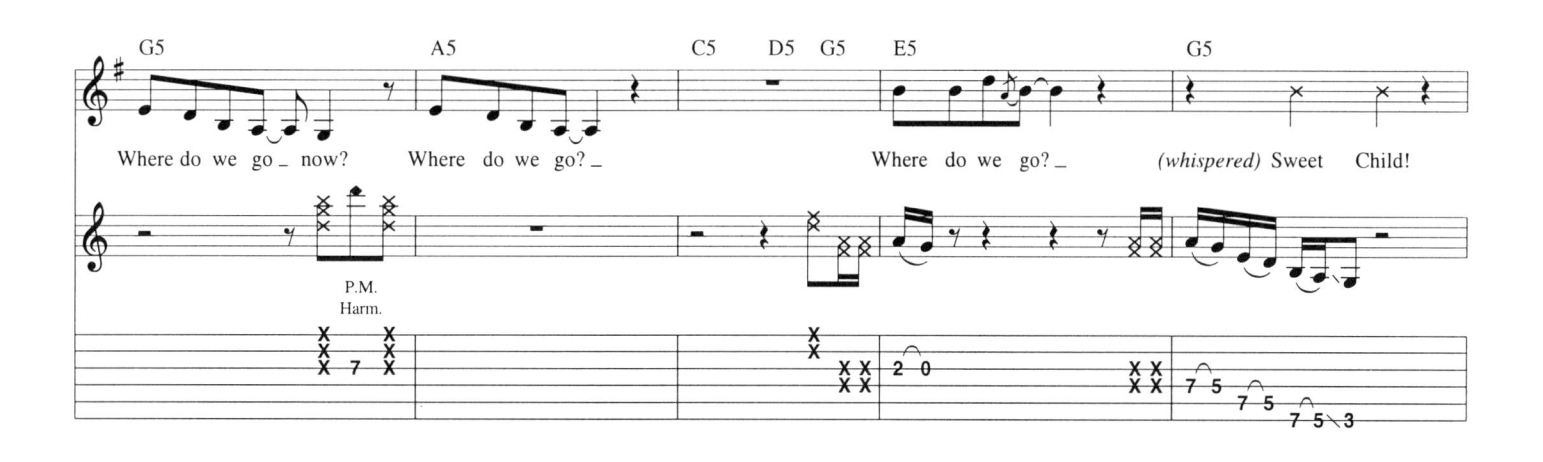

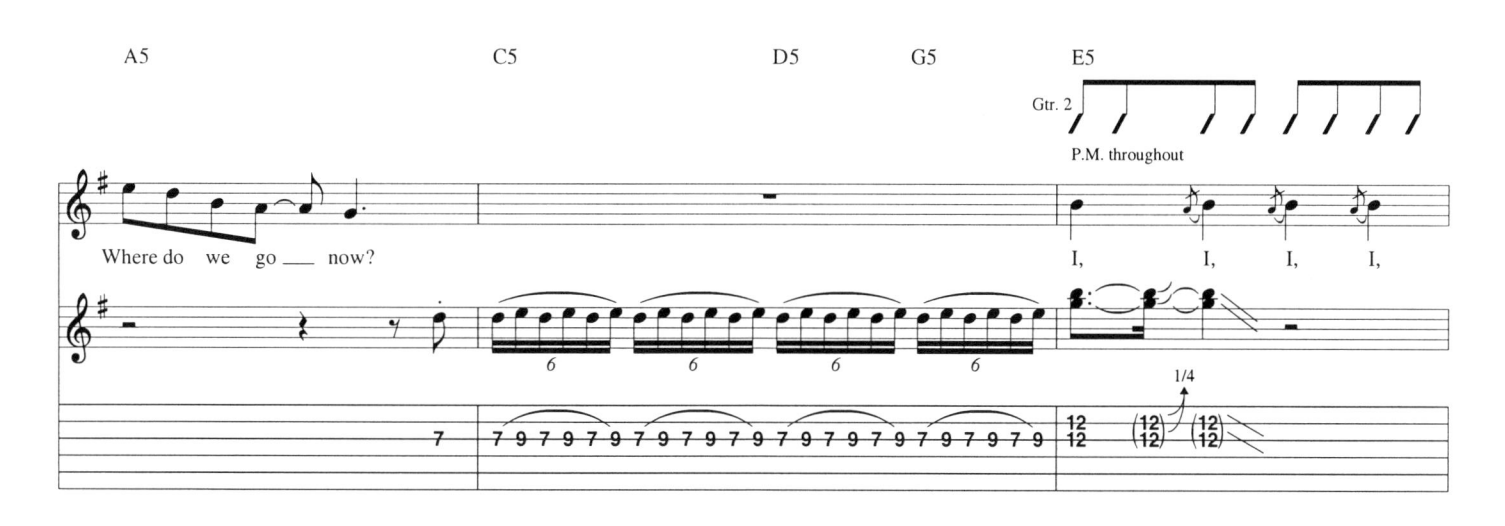

Where do we go? Where do we go now? Where do we go? Where do we go?

Where do we go now? Where do we go? Where do we go? *(whispered)* Sweet Child!

Where do we go now? I, I, I, I,

G5
A5
C5
D5V
G5III
I, I, I, I,
Where do we go now, now?
8va
full
E5
E ⑥ open
F♯ ⑥ 2fr
Rhy. Fig. 7
Where do we go?
Ah.
Where do we go now?
B5
End Rhy. Fig. 7
Gtr. 2: w/ Rhy. Fig. 7
When do we go?
loco
grad. bend full
1/2
Where do we go now?
D5

Gtr. 2: w/ Rhy. Fig. 7, first 3 meas.
E5 G5 A5 B5 E5 D5 B5 B♭5 A5 G
Gtr. 2
8va
Where do we go?
Where do we go now?
No, no, no, no, no, no,
grad. bend
full
1/2
Gtr. 2: w/ Rhy. Fig. 7, first 2 meas.
E5 A5 C5 D5
no. Sweet child, sweet child o'
E5
mine.
-1/2
Gtr. 4
Gtr. 1
divisi
*bend neck

You Give Love a Bad Name

Words and Music by Jon Bon Jovi, Richie Sambora and Desmond Child

Gtr. 2 tacet
N.C. (Cm)
Gtr. 1: w/ Fill 1, 2nd time
E♭5
1. An
2. You
Gtr. 1
Rhy. Fig. 1
End Rhy. Fig. 1
P.M.
w/ bar
-1/2
Verse
Gtr. 1: w/ Rhy. Fig. 1, 4 times
N.C. (Cm)
an-gel's smile is what you sell. You prom-ised me heav-en, then put me through hell.
paint your smile on your lips, blood - red nails on your fin - ger tips. A
Chains of love got a hold on me. When pas-sion's a pris-on you can't break free.
school boy's dream, you act so shy. Your ver - y first kiss was your first kiss good-bye.
Pre-Chorus
F5
E♭5
Whoa, you're a load - ed gun. Yeah.
Fill 1
Gtr. 1
T
A
B

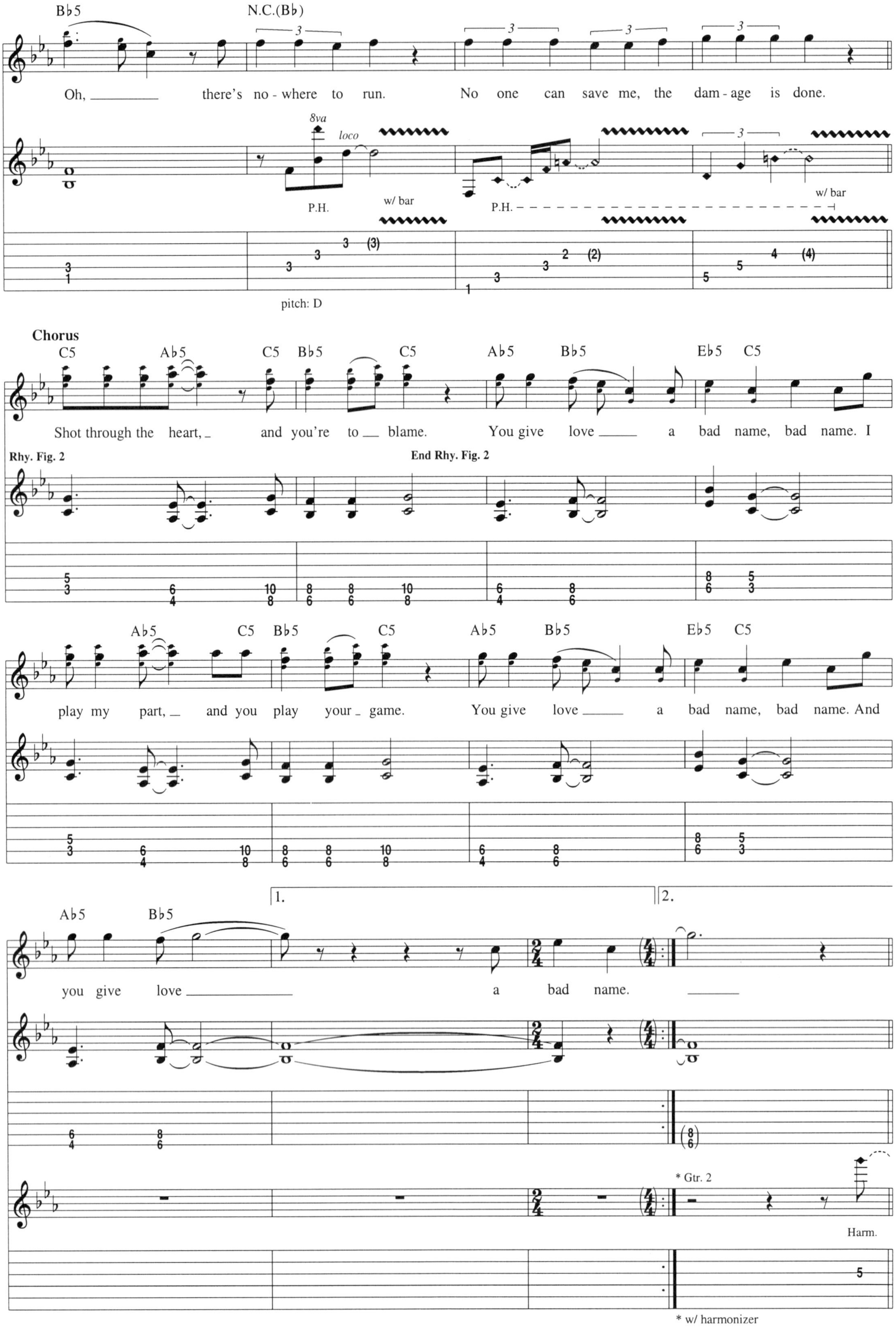

* w/ harmonizer

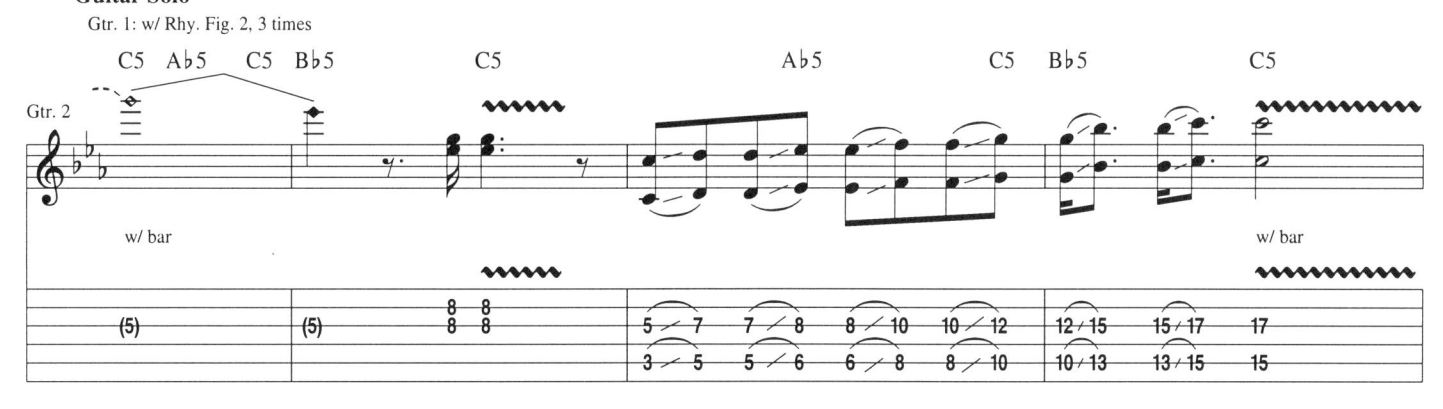

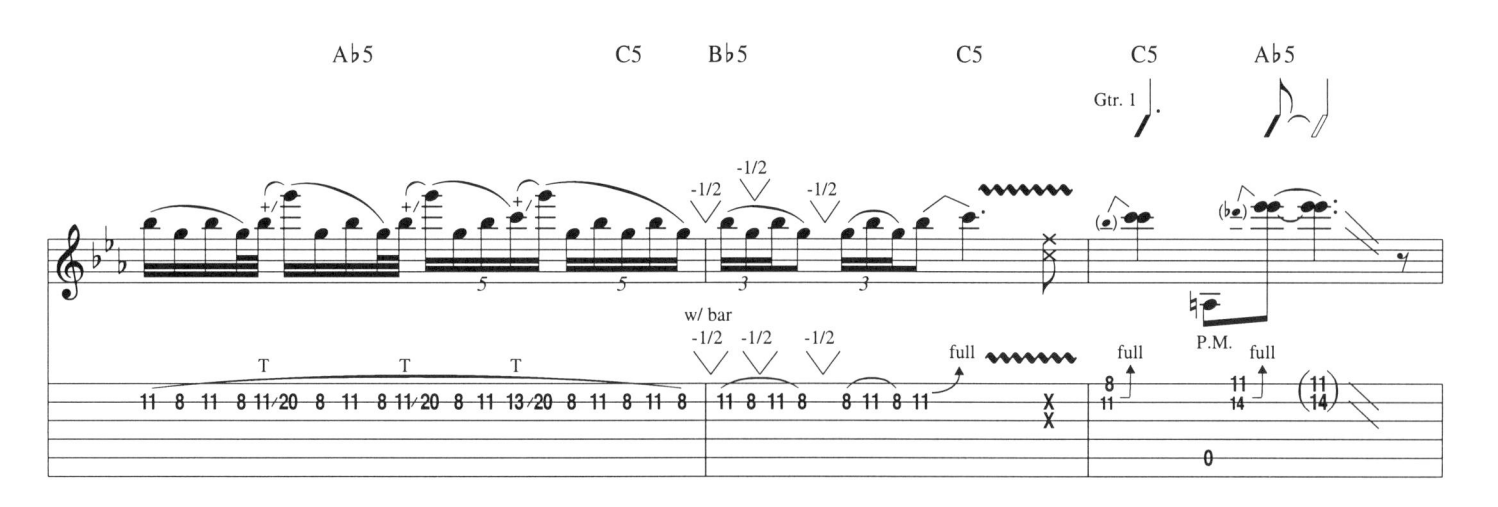

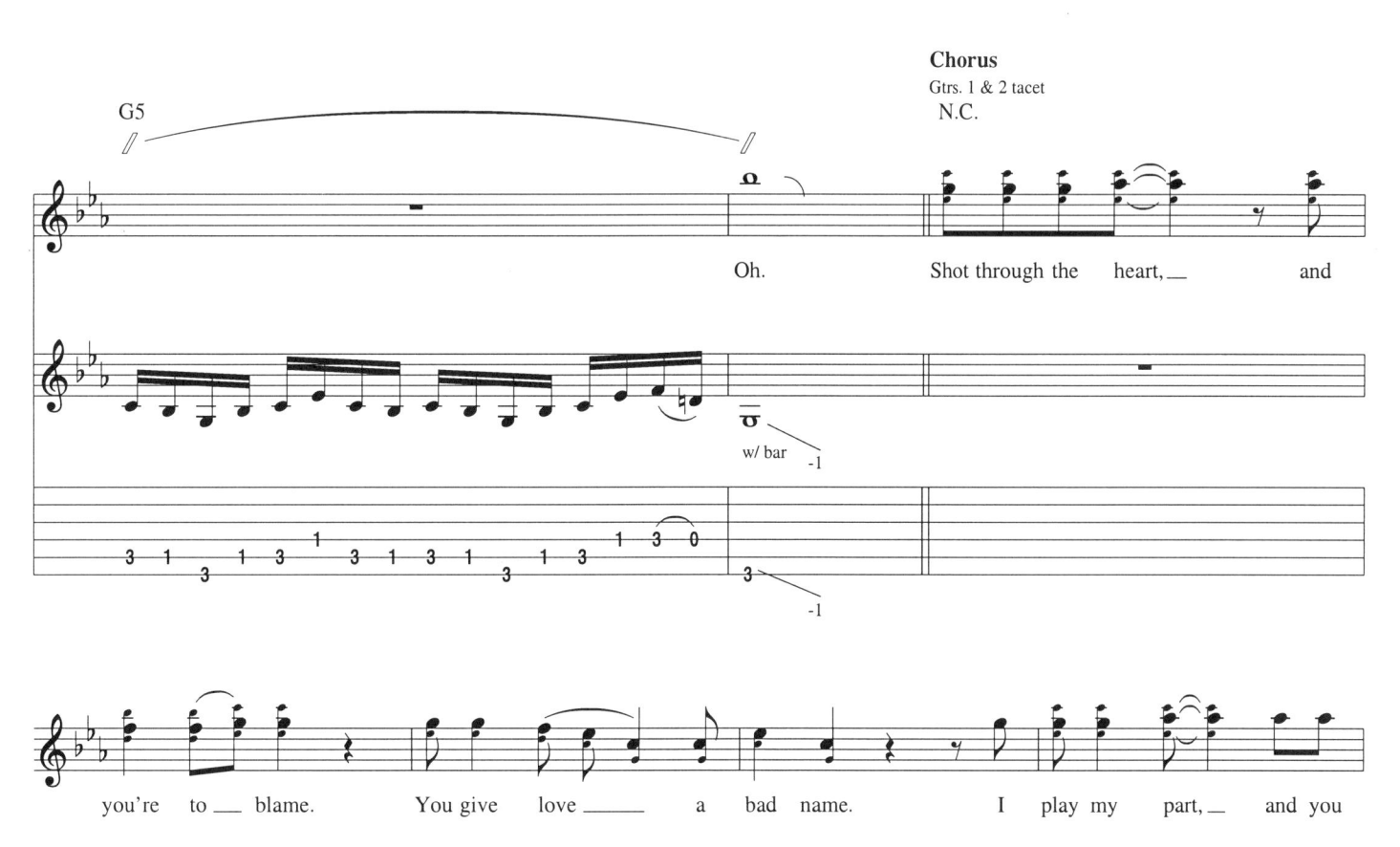

Guitar Solo
Gtr. 1: w/ Rhy. Fig. 2, 3 times

Chorus
Gtrs. 1 & 2 tacet
N.C.

Oh. Shot through the heart, and you're to blame. You give love a bad name. I play my part, and you play your game. You give love a bad name, bad name.

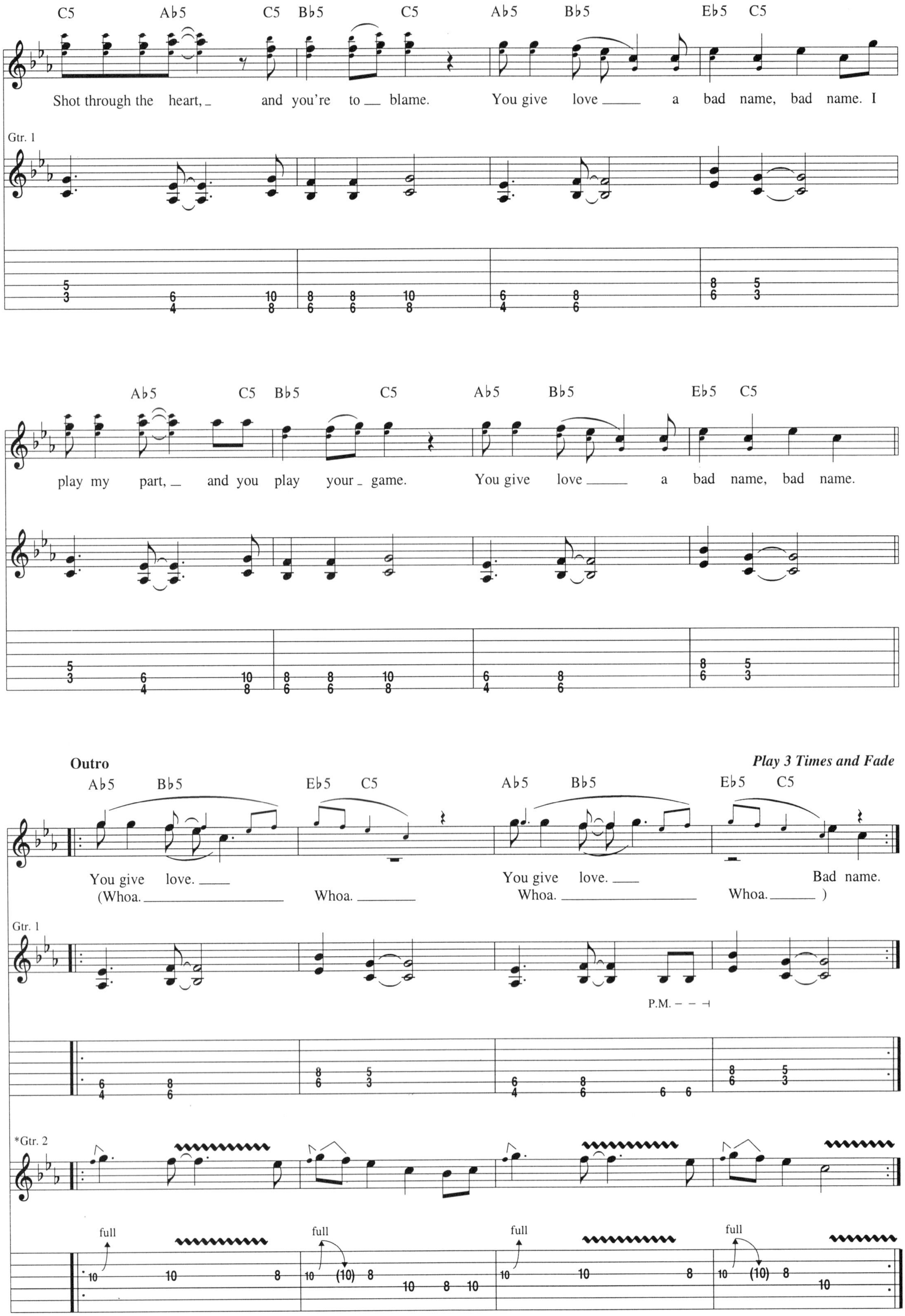

*w/ harmonizer

You Shook Me All Night Long

Words and Music by Angus Young, Malcolm Young and Brian Johnson

G C G D5 G D5 G D5
fight - in' for air, she told me to come, but I was al - read - y there. 'Cause the
oth - er round, now I'm back in the ring to take an - oth - er swing. That the
bass enters
G C G C G D *G/D D5 *G/D D5
walls start shak-in', the earth was quak-in', my mind was ach - in', and we were mak - in' it.
walls were shak-in', the earth was quak-in', my mind was ach - in', and we were mak - in' it. And
Gtrs. 1 & 2
*bass plays D
Chorus
G5 Cadd9 G/B D5 Cadd9 G/B
you shook me all night long. Yeah, you
Rhy. Fig. 2
End Rhy. Fig. 2
Gtrs. 1 & 2: w/ Rhy. Fig. 2
G5 Cadd9 G/B D5 Cadd9 G/B G/B
shook me all night long. 2nd time: (You) 2.Work-in' knock me out, I said,
1.
2.
Gtrs. 1 & 2: w/ Rhy. Fig. 2
G5 Cadd9 G/B D5 Cadd9 G/B
you shook me all night long. You had me shak-in', and
G5 Cadd9 G/B D5 G5/D
you shook me all night long.
Gtrs. 1 & 2

95

G5 Cadd9 G/B D5 Cadd9 G/B
You real - ly took me, and
8va
full 1/2 1/2 full full full
Outro-Chorus
Gtrs. 1 & 2: w/ Rhy. Fig. 2, 3 times
Gtr. 3 tacet
G5 Cadd9 G/B D5 Cadd9 G/B
you shook me all night long. Ah,
G5 Cadd9 G/B D5 Cadd9 G/B
you shook me all night long. Yeah, yeah, you
G5 Cadd9 G/B D5 Cadd9 G/B
shook me all night long! You real - ly got me, and
G5 Cadd9 G/B D Cadd9 G/B D
you shook me all night long! Yeah, you shook me,
Gtrs. 1 & 2
Cadd9 G/D D
yeah, you shook me all night long!